Second Language Testing for Student Evaluation and Classroom Research

Student Workbook

Second Language Testing for Student Evaluation and Classroom Research

Student Workbook

by

Greta Gorsuch

and

Dale Griffee

INFORMATION AGE PUBLISHING, INC.
Charlotte, NC • www.infoagepub.com

Library of Congress Cataloging-in-Publication Data

CIP record for this book is available from the Library of Congress
http://www.loc.gov

ISBNs: 978-1-64113-017-2 (Paperback)

   978-1-64113-018-9 (ebook)

Copyright © 2018 Information Age Publishing Inc.

All rights reserved. No part of this publication may be reproduced, stored in a retrieval system, or transmitted, in any form or by any means, electronic, mechanical, photocopying, microfilming, recording or otherwise, without written permission from the publisher.

Printed in the United States of America

STUDENT WORKBOOK CONTENTS

1. Norm-Referenced Tests *1*
2. Test Item Formats *11*
3. Teacher-Made Tests (CRTs)..*17*
4. The Role of Theory in Second-Language Testing *29*
5. Performance Tests.. *41*
6. Descriptive Statistics *55*
7. Correlation *69*
8. Reliability *91*
9. Validity and Validation *115*
10. Standard Setting and Cut Scores.. *123*
11. Tests and Teaching... *129*
12. Tests and Classroom Research *145*

STUDENT WORKBOOK
CHAPTER 1

NORM-REFERENCED TESTS

TEST YOURSELF

Working alone or with a study partner, ask and answer these questions:

1. What does TREE stand for?

2. What is a norming group?

3. What is Item Facility (IF)?

4. What is Item Discrimination (ID)?

5. What are five advantages of NRTs?

6. What are five disadvantages of NRTs?

7. What does the term SEM mean?

8. Explain what local validation means.

9. What is a measurement model?

10. What is domain theory? Can you think of an example?

DISCUSSION QUESTIONS

1. Under what conditions would you be happy that your students took a norm-referenced test (NRT) and that you had access to their scores?

2. Under what circumstances might you make an NRT?

3. Your school director wants to evaluate your language program. In a meeting, he suggests using a standardized test he can buy to measure students' proficiency when they enter the program and again when they leave. He believes these test scores will help students find a job. How do you respond?

4. You are working in a small language school. For some time, teachers have been complaining that their classes have mixed levels of students in them and that is making it hard for them to teach. The school director asks you for your advice to deal with this problem because she knows you have taken a testing course. She wishes to know whether you could make some kind of test that could be given to all new students to determine the level of the class to which they should be assigned. What are some possible recommendations you can make?

APPLICATION TASKS

1. An Item Facility (IF) is the percentage of items answered correctly. Calculate IFs for a simulated test with six students and seven items using the data in Table 1.1. The students (sometimes called test candidates) are in the first column. The next seven rows are scores for the students on each NRT item. If there is a 1, it means the student got the item right. If there is a 0, it means the student got the item wrong. Thus, for student 1, we can see that on item 1, she got the item right, but that on item 2 she got it wrong. This arrangement allows us to calculate and display IFs for each item. The formula is IF = $N_{correct} / N_{total}$. For item 1, the IF is .67 (4 divided by 6). In other words, 67% of the students got item 1 correct. Now, calculate the IFs for items 2 through 10.

2. Which items in Table 1.1 are easy? Which are in the middle? Which are difficult? Given the general guideline that good NRT items

have IFs between .2 and .8, which items would you keep? Why? Which items would you revise? Why?

3. Table 1.2 shows a different group of students who took an NRT with 100 total items. Using Table 1.2, calculate IFs and IDs for items 2 through 8. Note that the new group of students is now arranged in three levels by total score to identify IF upper and IF lower. For example, this means that Al (not his real name) got a total score of 85, calculated from adding up all of the correct answers from items 1 through 100 on. The lowest scoring student on the whole test was Ted. The formula is ID = $IF_{upper} - IF_{lower}$. Item 1 has been done for you. Note that 75% of the highest group answer item 1 correctly. Thus, the IF for the upper group is .75. Only 25% of the lowest group answered item 1 correctly, with an IF of .25. (75 minus .25 = .5, the ID for the item).

Table 1.1.
NRT Item-Level Data Arranged to Calculate Item Facility

Items	1	2	3	4	5	6	7	8	9	10, etc.
Student 1	1	0	1	1	1	1	1	0	1	0
Student 2	1	1	0	1	1	1	1	0	1	0
Student 3	1	0	1	0	1	1	0	0	1	1
Student 4	0	1	1	1	1	1	1	0	1	0
Student 5	1	0	0	1	1	1	0	0	1	0
Student 6	0	1	1	0	0	0	0	1	1	0
N correct	4									
N total	6									
IF =	.67									

Table 1.2.
NRT Items Arranged to Calculate Item Facility and Item Discrimination

Items	1	2	3	4	5	6	7	8, etc.	Total Score
Al	1	1	1	0	1	1	0	1	85
Wanda	1	1	1	0	0	1	0	0	82
Emily	1	1	0	0	1	1	0	0	81
Peter	0	1	1	0	1	1	0	1	80
Anna	1	1	1	0	1	0	0	1	75
Tom W.	0	1	0	1	0	1	0	1	74
Tom Z.	0	1	0	1	1	0	0	0	72
Neil	0	0	1	0	1	1	0	1	70
Joan	1	0	0	1	0	0	0	0	66
Shirley	0	1	0	0	1	0	0	0	65
Georgia	1	1	1	0	0	0	0	0	55
Jean	0	1	0	1	0	0	0	0	52
Kenny	0	1	0	0	0	0	1	0	50
Ted	0	1	0	1	0	0	1	0	48
IF_{upper}	.75								
IF_{lower}	.25								
ID	.50								

5. Which test items in Table 1.2 would you keep as good items? Why? Which items would you look at and revise? Why? How might you revise an item?
6. Following the format in Table 1.2, find item-level and total scores from an NRT test and calculate the IFs and IDs.

TEST YOURSELF ANSWERS

1. What does TREE stand for?
   Teacher/Researcher/Educator/Evaluator

2. What is a norming group?
   It's the group on which a norm-referenced (NRT) test is created.

3. What is Item Facility (IF)?
   An IF is the percentage of students who answer a test item correctly.

4. What is Item Discrimination (ID)?
   Item Discrimination shows the extent to which a test item separates high-scoring students from low-scoring students.

5. What are five advantages of NRTs?

   - They can measure language proficiency.
   - They level the playing field, meaning that the test is the same for all students.
   - Scores from an NRT can be used to characterize or describe students from a class.
   - We can buy an NRT from a test company.
   - A commercially produced NRT can include supplemental material such as practice test forms, CDs, and a test manual discussing the development of the test.

6. What are five disadvantages of NRTs?
   - They are a poor measure of learning in a particular program.
   - They require added test security.
   - Their scores have to be interpreted.
   - They measure traits, and traits are static and not dynamic.
   - They encourage belief that our knowledge is inborn rather than worked for.

7. What is an SEM?
   SEM stands for standard error of measurement and is a band around each person's NRT test score showing how high or low the score might actually be.

8. Explain what local validation means.
   Gathering evidence that the test measures your students accurately and appropriately.

9. What is a measurement model?
   A theory of underlying assumptions of a test.

10. What is domain theory?
    The theory of what the test (any test, not just an NRT) is purporting to measure. Domain theory examples include: (A) listening comprehension requires both top-down and bottom-up processing, (b) guessing unknown words from context is an important skill for independent reading, (c) learners writing in a foreign language need to learn to

write for different audiences, (d) communicative competence in speaking means knowing what to say depending on whom you are talking to and for what reason, and (e) the list is endless!

DISCUSSION QUESTIONS ANSWERS

1. Under what conditions would you be happy that your students took a norm-referenced test (NRT) and that you had access to their scores?

   When you want to make admissions or placement decisions, scores from an NRT is useful. Another use is comparing your students to other students in your program, past and present, who have also taken the test. This information may be used to project long-term responses you think your program should make in response to changes in the student population attending your school. Finally, if you want to determine that two or more groups of students are generally the same in language ability at the beginning of a research project, norm-reference test scores are useful.

2. Under what circumstances might you make an NRT?

   Some schools wish to make an NRT for admissions or placement to save money. There is also an argument that a placement test should have a stronger relationship to the program outcomes than commercially available NRTs generally do.

3. Your school director wants to evaluate your language program. In a meeting, he suggests using a standardized test he can buy to measure students' proficiency when they enter the program and again when they leave. He believes these test scores will help students find a job. How do you respond?

   The director has a point that graduates with high scores on a well-known NRT make a positive impression on prospective employers. However, an NRT should not be used to measure learning over time. Most NRTs will not detect improvement on well-defined program outcomes. Suggest to the director that a well-designed CRT be used to show learning over time, and report improvement in terms of the outcomes. Students can take the well-known NRT as an option to improve their job search portfolios.

4. You are working in a small language school. For some time, teachers have been complaining that their classes have mixed levels of students in them, and that is making it hard for them to teach. The school director asks you for your advice to deal with this problem

because she knows you have taken a testing course. She wishes to know whether you could make some kind of test that could be given to all new students to determine the level of the class to which they should be assigned. What are some possible recommendations you can make?

It is possible to buy or make an NRT to give to students when they start in a school. The scores can be used to make placement decisions. You may wish to suggest that you be paid extra or given teaching release to get consensus on the program outcomes, and then to find or make a placement NRT that has some relationship to the program outcomes.

APPLICATION TASKS ANSWERS

1. An IF (Item Facility) is the percentage of items answered correctly. Calculate IFs for a simulated test with six students and seven items using the data in Table 1.3. The students (sometimes called test candidates) are in the first column. The next seven rows are scores for the students on each NRT item. If there is a 1, it means the student got the item right. If there is a 0, it means the student got the item wrong. Thus, for student 1, we can see that on item 1, she got the item right, but that on item 2 she got it wrong. This arrangement allows us to calculate and display IFs for each item. The formula is IF = $N_{correct} / N_{total}$. For item 1, the IF is .67 (4 divided by 6). In other words, 67% of the students got item 1 correct. Now, calculate the IFs for items 2 through 10.

Table 1.3.
NRT Item-Level Data Arranged to Calculate Item Facility Answers

Items	1	2	3	4	5	6	7	8	9	10, etc.
Student 1	1	0	1	1	1	1	1	0	1	0
Student 2	1	1	0	1	1	1	1	0	1	0
Student 3	1	0	1	0	1	1	0	0	1	1
Student 4	0	1	1	1	1	1	1	0	1	0
Student 5	1	0	0	1	1	1	0	0	1	0
Student 6	0	1	1	0	0	0	0	1	1	0
N correct	4	3	4	4	5	5	3	1	6	1
N total	6	6	6	6	6	6	6	6	6	6
IF =	.67	.50	.67	.67	.83	.83	.50	.17	1.00	.17

2. Which items in Table 1.3 are easy? Which are in the middle? Which are difficult items? Given the general guideline that good NRT items have IFs between .2 and .8, which items would you keep? Why? Which items would you revise? Why?
Items 5, 6, and 9 are easy for the students. Items 1, 2, 3, 4, and 7 are in the middle. Items 8 and 10 are difficult for students. Items 1, 2, 3, 4, and 7 are within the suggested range and should be retained. Items 5, 6, and 9 are too easy, whereas items 8 and 10 are too difficult. Thus, the items may not function to spread students out on a score continuum. These five items should be revised.
3. Table 1.4 shows a different group of students who took an NRT with 100 total items. Using Table 1.4, calculate IFs and IDs for items 2 through 8. Note that the new group of students is now arranged in three levels by total score to identify IF upper and IF lower. For example, this means that Al (not his real name) got a total score of 85, calculated from adding up all of the correct answers from items 1 through 100 on. The lowest scoring student on the whole test was Ted. The formula is ID = $IF_{upper} - IF_{lower}$. Item 1 has been done for you. Note that 75% of the highest group answer item 1 correctly. Thus, the IF for the upper group is .75. Only 25% of the lowest group answered item 1 correctly, with an IF of .25 (.75 − .25 = .5, the ID for the item).

Table 1.4.
NRT Items Arranged to Calculate Item Facility and Item Discrimination Answers

Items	1	2	3	4	5	6	7	8, etc.	Total Score
Al	1	1	1	0	1	1	0	1	85
Wanda	1	1	1	0	0	1	0	0	82
Emily	1	1	0	0	1	1	0	0	81
Peter	0	1	1	0	1	1	0	1	80
Anna	1	1	1	0	1	0	0	1	75
Tom W.	0	1	0	1	0	1	0	1	74
Tom Z.	0	1	0	1	1	0	0	0	72
Neil	0	0	1	0	1	1	0	1	70
Joan	1	0	0	1	0	0	0	0	66

(Table continues on next page)

Table 1.4. (Continued)

Items	1	2	3	4	5	6	7	8, etc.	Total Score
Shirley	0	1	0	0	1	0	0	0	65
Georgia	1	1	1	0	0	0	0	0	55
Jean	0	1	0	1	0	0	0	0	52
Kenny	0	1	0	0	0	0	1	0	50
Ted	0	1	0	1	0	0	1	0	48
IF_{upper}	.75	1.00	.75	.00	.75	1.00	.00	.50	
IF_{lower}	.25	1.00	.25	.50	.00	.00	.50	.00	
ID	.50	.00	.50	−.50	.75	1.00	−.50	.50	

4. Which test items in Table 1.4 would you keep as good items? Why? Which items would you look at and revise? Why? How might you revise an item?
   Items with IDs above .20 are 1, 3, 5, 6, and 8. These items are effective to discriminate between high- and low-scoring students, as measured by their total test scores. Items 2, 4, and 7 do not discriminate between high- and low-scoring students. Item 2 appears to be easy for both high- and low-scoring students, and so the item might be made more difficult for low- scoring students. Items 4 and 7 need to have their wording checked. Something about the wording or the test directions is throwing the high-scoring students off and somehow benefitting the low-scoring students.
5. Following the format in Table 1.4, find item-level and total scores from an NRT test and calculate the IFs and IDs.

STUDENT WORKBOOK
CHAPTER 2

TEST ITEM FORMATS

TEST YOURSELF

Working alone or with a study partner, ask and answer these questions:

1. What is a test?
2. What is a test item?
3. What is a test item format?
4. What is a receptive format?
5. What is a productive format?
6. What are three receptive TIFs?
7. What are three productive TIFs?
8. What is a construct?
9. What is an analytic scale?
10. What is a holistic scale?

DISCUSSION QUESTIONS

1. If you are currently teaching, where did you get your test (or tests)? Is it clear to you what the TIFs are? What aspect of students' learning do you think your "inherited" tests are tapping into? In other words, what are the constructs?

2. Is there a TIF you feel particularly drawn to? Why?

3. What TIF do you think your teacher in this testing class should use? Why?

APPLICATION TASK

Find a test, describe it, and bring it to class.

What is the name of the test? _____

What is the name of the course the test is used in?_____

What is the particular objective or objectives of the course this test was designed to capture? _____
_____

How many items does the test have? _____

How many TIFs were used? _____

TIF #1 name_____ What was the percent of use?_____

TIF #2 name_____ What was the percent of use?_____

TIF #3 name_____ What was the percent of use?_____

Select one of the TIFs above. What knowledge or skill (the construct) is the TIF measuring?_____
_____
_____

What are the strong and weak points of the TIF?_____
_____

TEST YOURSELF ANSWERS

1. What is a test?
   A test is a document to measure knowledge or ability. It may be paper and pencil or electronic. A test is created for a purpose and produces data (test scores) from which inferences can be made about the purpose.

2. What is a test item?
   A test item is a question or statement on a test that requires a response from the test-taker.

3. What is a test item format (TIF)?
   The way a test item is answered on a test.

4. What is a receptive format?
   A receptive format, also known as a selected-response format, is a TIF that asks the test-taker to choose from answers provided by the test.

5. What is a productive format?
   A productive test item format requires the test-taker to produce or construct the answer.

6. What are three receptive TIFs?
   Multiple choice, true false, and matching items.

7. What are three productive TIFs?
   Fill in the blank, short responses, and tasks.

8. What is a construct?
   The knowledge, skill, or theoretical ability you are seeking to measure with a test. For example, if you are interested in a norm-referenced test that claims to measure language proficiency, then language proficiency is the construct.

9. What is an analytic scale?
   A rating scale based on objective descriptions of constructs or criteria.

10. What is a holistic scale?
    A rating scale based on criteria stated as a single statement.

APPLICATION TASK ANSWERS

Find a test, describe it, and bring it to class.

What is the name of the test?
If no name is used, ask for the name from the test writer or create a name that accurately describes the test.

What is the name of the course the test is used in?
Get the precise course name.

What is the particular objective or objectives of the course this test was designed to capture?
This can be found on the course syllabus or course description. If no objectives are named, ask the test writer or instructors of the course about the course objectives. Examples from a first semester college-level Japanese course are:

Students completing this course will be able to communicate orally at the ACTFL Novice high level or at the Common European Framework of Reference for Languages (CEFRL) level A2.

The student will acquire a vocabulary of about 400 words and 90 Kanji characters.

The student will learn functional tasks such as those listed below in the specific goals.

The student will be able to interpret, express and negotiate meaning, and communicate appropriately by using Japanese in the Japanese culture.

How many items does the test have?
Recall that an item is a question or statement that test candidates respond to, and where the response is scored. Thus, a test may have only two items if the TIF being used is short response or a task. A test using true/false or fill-in-the-blank TIFs may have a larger number of items.

How many TIFs were used?
Ask a classmate to check and confirm your answer.

TIF #1 name_____   What was the percent of use?_____

TIF #2 name_____   What was the percent of use?_____

TIF #3 name_____   What was the percent of use?_____

Confirm your answers with a classmate or colleague.

Select one of the TIFs above. What knowledge or skill (the construct) is the TIF measuring?
Show the sample items to a classmate or colleague and explain what you think the construct is.

What are the strong and weak points of the TIF?
Answers can focus on several points: (a) the extent to which the TIF can capture a given construct, (b) the extent to which the TIF reflects a course objective (if the test is a classroom test designed to show students' learning), (c) the extent to which a TIF can be credibly and reliably scored, and (d) the extent to which a TIF is communicative.

STUDENT WORKBOOK
CHAPTER 3

TEACHER-MADE TESTS (CRTs)

TEST YOURSELF

Working alone or with a study partner, ask and answer these questions:

1. What does CRT stand for?
2. What does mastery mean?
3. What is a criterion and is it singular or plural?
4. What is a construct? What are three examples?
5. What are five differences between NRTs and CRTs?
6. What is a histogram?
7. What is different between a histogram of an NRT, and a histogram of a CRT administered at the end of a unit or course?
8. What are two advantages of CRTs? What are two disadvantages of CRTs?
9. What is the difference between formative evaluation and summative evaluation?

10. What is an IF? What does it tell us?

11. What is a DI? What does it tell us?

12. What is a B-index? What does it tell us?

13. How can you check a CRT for reliability?

14. What some strategies for CRT validation?

15. What some reasons you might write a report on your test? What information do you need to include?

16. What is an item bank?

DISCUSSION QUESTIONS

1. Look again at the IFs and DIs in Table 3.6 in the textbook. Confirm the outcomes (1, 2, 3, or 4) suggested in the textbook Table 3.5. What are the ways you can explain the low DI items? For the items that need it, can you suggest possible revision strategies?

2. Collect one or two classroom tests from your own classes and/or from colleagues. How would you classify the tests (CRT or NRT) according to Table 3.1 in the textbook? If you are not sure, what questions could you ask the test writer(s) to clarify, according to Table 3.1?

3. Using the classroom tests from Discussion Question 2, think through the relationship between the test item formats used in the test and the constructs for the tests. Using steps 2 and 3 in the section "How can I make my own CRT?", are there other test item formats that can be used to capture the constructs?

4. How many of CRTs that you have made do you still have? Given the 12 steps for making a CRT, it is clear that constructing a good CRT takes time. Do you think you might be keeping more of your CRTs to reuse? Why or why not?

APPLICATION TASKS

1. Calculate a B-index. The cut point is represented by the line. Recall IF = students getting the test right/the number of students attempting the item. Thus, IF pass for item 1 is 4 / 5 = .80 (see Table 3.1).

Table 3.1.
Student Workbook CRT Item Analysis Assignment

I.D.	Item 1	Item 2	Item 3	Item 4	Item 5	Item 6	Item 7	Item 8	Item 9	Item 10	Total
S4	1	1	1	1	1	1	1	1	1	1	10
S2	1	1	1	0	1	1	1	1	1	1	9
S9	1	1	1	0	1	1	1	1	1	1	9
S8	1	1	1	1	0	0	1	1	1	1	8
S11	0	1	1	0	1	1	1	1	1	1	8
										pass $n = 5$	
										fail $n = 7$	
S1	1	0	1	0	1	0	1	0	1	0	5
S5	0	0	1	1	0	0	1	1	0	1	5
S7	0	0	0	0	0	1	1	1	1	1	5
S12	1	0	1	0	1	0	1	0	1	0	5
S6	0	1	0	0	1	1	0	1	0	0	4
S10	0	0	1	1	0	0	1	0	0	1	4
S3	0	1	0	0	0	0	1	0	0	0	2
IFpass											
IFfail											
B-index											

2. Collect a CRT from your own collection or from a colleague. Some CRTs can be found as unit reviews or actual achievement tests in the teacher's manual for a textbook. Answer these questions:

- What is the stated purpose of the test? What do you think is the purpose of the test?

- Is the test high stakes (fail this test and you either fail the course or get a low grade) or low stakes (test not scored, scores not recorded, or if they are, just one score among many)?

- What do you think are the constructs in the test? Try to explain the construct to a colleague. Did they understand your explanation, or did they offer an alternate explanation? What was it?

- Looking at the test, what would you guess the test domain is? Where do you think the domain came from?

- Looking only at the test, what do you believe the course objectives are? If you can, find the course syllabus or ask the colleague who made the test, what the course the course objectives are?

- How does the test relate to course objectives? Compare your judgments from before and after you learned about the course outcomes.

- Who wrote the items, and who reviews and revises the items? Given what you know about CRTs, test item formats, domains, and constructs, what are some suggestions you can make about revising two of the items?

TEST YOURSELF ANSWERS

1. What does CRT stand for?
   Criterion-referenced test.

2. What does mastery mean?
   Knowing something.

3. What is a criterion, and is it singular or plural?
   Criterion is singular and criteria are plural. A criterion is a standard by which something is judged.

4. What is a construct? What are three examples?
   Learners' knowledge, skills, or attitudes that a test is designed to capture. One reflecting knowledge skill is knowing the form for a business e-mail. Another reflecting skill is the ability to read L2 texts quickly and with good word identification. A third reflecting attitude is confidence to use the L2 to order food and talk with the wait staff in a restaurant.

5. What are five differences between NRTs and CRTs?
   There are many differences found in Table 3.1, but a sample of them includes: NRTs compare students to each other, and CRTs compare students to the course material (CRTs show what students have learned. NRTs emphasize differences between students, and CRTs emphasize grouping students in terms of course objectives they have improved on.

NRTs are mainly liked by administrators, while CRTs are mainly liked by classroom teachers.

NRTs are used to make admission and placement decisions, and CRTs are used to show achievement and to diagnose or detect progress or continuing areas of uncertainty.

A good NRT item is one that some students get wrong, and some students get right. A good CRT item is one that most students initially get wrong, and then later get right.

6. What is a histogram?

As histogram is a way of visually arranging scores from a distribution using continuous or interval data. In a language testing context, a horizontal axis is generally the scores on a test from zero to the highest score. On a vertical axis is the frequency or scores (the number of test candidates getting a particular total score).

7. What is the difference between a histogram of an NRT and a histogram of a CRT administered at the end of a unit or course?

The histogram for an NRT that is functioning well will reveal a normal distribution centered around a mean, and with about the same number of test candidates getting scores below the mean and above the mean. The histogram for an end-of-unit CRT should be bunched up toward the right (negative skewness), meaning most students got high scores. The peak of the histogram (showing the mean score) will be high and narrow, and it is not necessarily the case that an equal number of students got scores above and below the mean.

8. What are two advantages of CRTs? What are two disadvantages of CRTs?

One advantage is CRTs describe what a student can do in terms of course objectives. A second advantage is what a CRT directly measures the amount of knowledge or skill a student has. There are several other advantages. One <u>dis</u>advantage is that CRTs may be idiosyncratic to individual teachers who may not be clear what they wish to measure. A second disadvantage is that CRTs may not comfortably fit an A, B, C, D, F grading system because they focus on pass/fail distinctions.

9. What is the difference between formative evaluation and summative evaluation? Can a CRT be used for both types?

Formative evaluation is done during the course and summative evaluation is done after the course is finished. A CRT can be used for both types of evaluation because a CRT is designed to diagnose (useful for formative evaluation) and show progress or achievement (useful for both formative and summative evaluation).

10. What is an IF? What does it tell us?
An Item Facility (IF) is the percentage of students who answered a certain item correctly. The formula for the IF is the number of items scored correct divided by the total number of items. If an IF is high (.5 to 1.00) it means an item was easy for test candidates. If an IF is low (0 to .49) it means an item was difficult for test candidates.

11. What is a DI? What does it tell us?
The Difference Index (DI) is the change in easiness or difficulty of an item over time. The formula is IF posttest minus IF pretest for an item, which assumes that a teacher gives the CRT as a pretest, but then also as a posttest. One hopes that as students learn from a course, they will find test items easier to answer because they have learned the course content. A DI of .1 to 1.00 indicates that on the posttest, test candidates found the item easier to answer than they did in the pretest. Items with DIs of −1.00 to .09 need to be examined and revised or thrown out.

12. What is a B-index?
The B-index is similar to the DI, but instead of measuring the difference of item easiness and difficulty between the pre-test and post-test, it assumes a single test administration. The formula is IF passing minus IF failing. The B-index tells us how masters (students who passed the test) and non-masters (students who failed the test) experienced a test item. If a B-index is high (.2 to 1.00) it indicates passing students found the item easy to answer but failing students found it difficult to answer. If a B-index is low (−1.00 to .19) it indicates that either: passing or failing students did not find the item easy, or that failing students somehow how the item easy while passing students did not.

13. How can you check a CRT for reliability?
You can use a classical NRT approach, such as KR-21 or Cronbach's alpha, if the distribution of the test scores is not completely non-normal. You can also use phi lambda, which does not assume a normal distribution. You can build reliability into a CRT by writing the ideas carefully, and putting a lot of thought sampling the domain of the course and thinking through what knowledge or skills you wish to capture.

14. What are some strategies for CRT validation?
    One is doing an intervention study where you give a pretest, teach the course, and then give a posttest. The extent to which students showed improvement (many items with high DIs) is the extent to which your test successfully measured the knowledge and skills of interest. A second is reporting CRT item analyses, highlighting high DI items and high B-index items. A third is defining the constructs of your test and showing the constructs and sample items to colleagues for comment. A fourth is reporting on content validity of the test.

15. What are some reasons you might write a report on your test? What information do you need to include?
    Accountability to others is one reason, and another is to keep the information on hand so you can do future revisions of the test. Important parts of a test report are an actual copy of the test, data from item analyses, a diary of your test development and administration process, and information on the group you administered the test to.

16. What is an item bank?
    An item bank is the storage of all items created for a test whether they were used or not.

DISCUSSION QUESTIONS ANSWERS

1. Look again at the IFs and DIs in Table 3.6 in the textbook. Confirm the outcomes (1, 2, 3, or 4) suggested in the text using Table 3.5. What are the ways you can explain the low DI items? For the items that need it, can you suggest possible revision strategies?

Although none of the items is highly functioning, items 2, 4, 5, and 10 are not working, and revision would probably start with these items. Without the actual test, it is not possible to suggest revision (see Table 3.2).

Table 3.2.
Student Workbook Possible Pretest and Posttest CRT Item-Level Outcomes

Item	Outcome	Possible Revision Strategy
2	2	Both pre- and posttest IFs are high, suggesting the item is too easy; make the item harder and check relationship to the course curriculum.
4	2	Both pre- and posttest IFs are high, suggesting the item is too easy; at the same time, there is little change from the pre- to the posttest, so check to see whether the item is related to the course curriculum.
5	1	More students got the item right on the pre-test than on the posttest, suggesting the item is not reliable. Check the wording and/or the instructions, and check whether the item is related to the course curriculum.
10	2	Both pre- and posttest IFs are high, suggesting the item is too easy; at the same time, there is little change from the pre- to the posttest, so check to see whether the item is related to the course curriculum.

2. Collect one or two classroom tests from your own classes and/or from colleagues. How would you classify the tests (CRT or NRT) according to Table 3.1 in the textbook? If you are not sure, what questions could you ask the test writer(s) to clarify, according to Table 3.1?
Possible questions to ask the test writer are: What do you use this test for? What do the students' scores mean? Are the students' scores reported as a percentage? Do you return the tests to the students and discuss the results? Do you use the scores to plan your lessons? How many times do you administer the students during the course? Why? At what point in the course do you administer the test? Why then?

3. Using the classroom tests from Discussion Question 2, think through the relationship between the test item formats used in the test and the constructs for the tests. Using steps 3 and 3 in the section "How can I make my own CRT?", are there other test item formats that can be used to capture the constructs?
Without seeing the tests in question, it is not possible to provide an answer. However, many TREEs find that, with thought, they can expand the type and appropriateness of test item formats they typically use. They may also find they do not adequately sample the course domain and content, perhaps using only more recent content, and not content the learners engaged with in the early stages of the course or unit.

4. How many of CRTs that you have made do you still have? Given the 12 steps for making a CRT, it is clear that constructing a good CRT takes time. Do you think you might be keeping more of your CRTs to reuse? Why or why not?
   Like student worksheets and other materials that teachers make, CRTs are not kept and reused. This may be an effect of local teacher theory, discussed in Chapter 4 (The Role of Theory), which is fluid, suited to teachers' conceptions of students' immediate needs and interests, and not often open to introspection. Nonetheless, to make a good CRT takes thinking that is somewhat outside of local teacher theory. Consider keeping worksheets and CRTs, and analyzing and reusing them.

APPLICATION TASKS ANSWERS

1. Calculate a B-index

Table 3.3.
Student Workbook CRT Item Analysis Assignment Answers

I.D.	Item 1	Item 2	Item 3	Item 4	Item 5	Item 6	Item 7	Item 8	Item 9	Item 10	Total
S4	1	1	1	1	1	1	1	1	1	1	10
S2	1	1	1	0	1	1	1	1	1	1	9
S9	1	1	1	0	1	1	1	1	1	1	9
S8	1	1	1	1	0	0	1	1	1	1	8
S11	0	1	1	0	1	1	1	1	1	1	8
											pass $n = 5$
											fail $n = 7$
S1	1	0	1	0	1	0	1	0	1	0	5
S5	0	0	1	1	0	0	1	1	0	1	5
S7	0	0	0	0	0	1	1	1	1	1	5
S12	1	0	1	0	1	0	1	0	1	0	5
S6	0	1	0	0	1	1	0	1	0	0	4
S10	0	0	1	1	0	0	1	0	0	1	4
S3	0	1	0	0	0	0	1	0	0	0	2
IFpass	.80	1.00	1.00	.40	.80	.80	1.00	1.00	1.00	1.00	
IFfail	.29	.29	.57	.29	.43	.29	.86	.43	.43	.43	
B-index	.51	.71	.43	.11	.37	.51	.14	.57	.57	.57	

Keep in mind:

- Reporting is rounded to two decimal points.
- Coefficients should be read as *point three three,* not as thirty three percent.
- According to Table 3.8 in the textbook, the following items are good and should be kept: 1, 2, 3, 5, 6, 8, 9, and 10. Items 4 and 7 need to be revised.

2. Collect a CRT from your own collection or from a colleague. Some CRTs can be found as unit reviews or actual achievement tests in the teacher's manual for a textbook. Answer these questions:

- What is the stated purpose of the test? What do you think is the purpose of the test?
  The two answers may not be the same.

- Is the test high stakes (fail this test and you either fail the course or get a low grade), or low stakes (test not scored, scores not recorded, or if they are, just one score among many)?
  It is unknown what answer you will find.

- What do you think are the constructs in the test? Try to explain the construct to a colleague. Did they understand your explanation, or did they offer an alternate explanation? What was it?
  As with the first question for application task 2, you may get a variety of answers.

- Looking at the test, what would you guess the test domain is? Where do you think the domain came from?
  It is unknown what answer you will find.

- Looking only at the test, what do you believe the course objectives are? If you can, find the course syllabus or ask the colleague who made the test, what the course objectives are.
  You may get conflicting answers.

- How does the test relate to course objectives? Compare your judgments from before and after you learned about the course outcomes.
  It is unknown what answer you will find.

- Who wrote the items, and who reviews and revises the items? Given what you know about CRTs, test item formats, domains, and constructs, what are some suggestions you can make about revising two of the items?
  It is unknown what answer you will find.

STUDENT WORKBOOK
CHAPTER 4

THE ROLE OF THEORY IN SECOND-LANGUAGE TESTING

TEST YOURSELF

Working alone or with a study partner, ask and answer these questions:

1. What are some reasons teachers avoid theory or dislike theory?

2. What does a theory do?

3. What are three theories relevant to second language learning and teaching mentioned in the chapter or that you are familiar with?

4. What are three forms theories can take?

5. What is an inductive approach to theory? What are three types of research using an inductive approach to theory?

6. What is a deductive approach to theory? What is the one type of research using a deducting approach to theory?

7. What does HML stand for?

8. What is grand theory or high-level theory? What is an example?

9. What is domain theory or middle-level theory? What is an example?

10. What is teacher theory or low-level theory? What is an example?

11. What kind of theory is communicative competence?

12. What is grammatical competence?

13. What is sociolinguistic competence?

14. What is textual competence?

15. What is pragmatic competence?

16. What is strategic competence?

17. What are the four features of a communicative activity or task?

18. What are the four features of a communicative test?

DISCUSSION QUESTIONS

1. How would you describe your attitude toward theory? Where do you think your attitude comes from?

2. As if to a nonapplied linguist, how would you explain the difference between the two high-level theories of language proficiency and communicative competence?

3. Why would communicative competence be a high-level theory and not just a middle-level theory such as the Output Hypothesis?

4. What are some middle-level theories about language learning or teaching that you know? Can you explain the theories to others?

5. What is one thing you believe, as a language learner or a language teacher, about language learning? This may be an example of low theory or teacher theory.

Second Language Testing for Student Evaluation and Classroom Research   31

6. As a language *learner* you took tests. Were the tests communicative or do you think they focused on grammatical competence? What makes you think so?

7. How would our beliefs as a language *learner* affect our beliefs as a *teacher*?

8. Is it always necessary that every classroom test be 100% communicative? Are there times when non-communicative tests or subtests are appropriate? If so, what would be three to four examples?

APPLICATION TASKS

1. If you are teaching, list three pedagogical practices you use in your class; if you are not teaching, list three pedagogical practices you have experienced as a student or seen used. Describe each and identify the teaching methodology (and the theory or belief) that supports these practices?

   Your practices as a teacher: Practices you experienced as a student:

   _____   _____

   _____   _____

   _____   _____

2. Using your own test or a test your colleague would be kind enough to show you, what do you think is the test purpose? How do you know? What constructs do you see? Ask a classmate and confirm or disconfirm your impressions. How do the test items measure the constructs? Is there a TIF that might be more effective? Is the test communicative? How so?

3. Here is part of a teacher-made test. What do you believe is the purpose of the test? What constructs do you see? Ask a classmate or colleague and confirm or disconfirm your impressions. Is the test communicative? How so?

Test Directions and Audio Script:

Please clear your tables and take out a pencil and an eraser. If you cannot hear this recording, please raise your hand now.

This is a test for More HearSay. *Please write your name at the top of the page and write your student number. Please write the date the same way as is on the board. I will now stop the tape so you may write your name, your student number and the date.*

Name _____ Student number _____

Partial More HearSay Test V.3. (Griffee, 1992)   Date_____

Task 1. Listen and write only the numbers you hear.

1. _____
2. _____
3. _____
4. _____
5. _____
6. _____

Task 1 Audio script (learners do not see this, they only hear it):
Listen and write only the numbers you hear. Do not write the sentence.

1. *Can you help me? I have to make twenty-five copies of this report.*
   Can you help me? I have to make twenty-five copies of this report.
2. *Well, let's see. Sea mail costs forty cents and takes about a month.*
   Well, let's see. Sea mail costs forty cents and takes about a month.
3. *My telephone number is 386-2256.*
   My telephone number is 386-2256.
4. *And my extension is 211. Tell him to call me when he gets in.*
   And my extension is 211. Tell him to call me when he gets in.
5. *Would you tell Bob I need four thousand chips ASAP.*
   Would you tell Bob I need four thousand chips ASAP.
6. *A new car today will cost over ten thousand, easily.*
   A new car today will cost over ten thousand, easily.

Task 2. Listen and write only the prices you hear.

7. _____
8. _____
9. _____

10. _____
11. _____
12. _____

Task 2 Audio script (learners do not see this, they only hear it):
Listen and write only the prices you hear.

7. *Is fifty-four cents enough for an airmail letter to France?*
   Is fifty-four cents enough for an airmail letter to France?
8. *These new sweaters just came in. They're sixty-nine ninety-five.*
   These new sweaters just came in. They're sixty-nine ninety-five.
9. *Here you are. That'll be ninety cents, please.*
   Here you are. That'll be ninety cents, please.
10. *Let me see. Two eggs, toast and coffee is three seventy-five.*
    Let me see. Two eggs, toast and coffee is three seventy-five.
11. *A ticket for the bus is fourteen fifty. You can pay the driver.*
    A ticket for the bus is fourteen fifty. You can pay the driver.
12. *Deductible means if you have an accident, you have to pay the first two thousand dollars and the insurance pays the rest.*
    Deductible means if you have an accident, you have to pay the first two thousand dollars and the insurance pays the rest.

Task 3. Listen and circle the word you hear.

13.	that	to	I'll	this
14.	or	to	you'd	can you
15.	going to	aren't you	where do you	you could
16.	may	could	going	is
17.	been to	it's	I've	could you
18.	don't	the	a	that

Task 3 Audio script (learners do not see this, they only hear it):
Listen and circle the word you hear.

13. *You copy and I'll collate.*
    You copy and I'll collate.
14. *I want it to go airmail.*
    I want it to go airmail.
15. *You're flying to New York, aren't you?*
    You're flying to New York, aren't you?
16. *When's he coming back?*
    When's he coming back?

17. *You ever been to Hawaii?*
    You ever been to Hawaii?
18. *What's the matter?*
    What's the matter?

TEST YOURSELF ANSWERS

1. What are some reasons teachers avoid or dislike theory?
   We named: (a) Theories are referred to by many terms; (b) there are so many theories, and they appear chaotic, random, and contradictory; (c) teachers do not think theories are written for them; (d) few teacher training programs teach theory; (e) teachers do not have experience discussing theory as it relates to their practice; and (f) the institutions where teachers work do not necessarily value theory.

2. What does a theory do?
   A theory explains phenomena.

3. What are three theories relevant to second-language learning and teaching mentioned in the chapter?
   We list quite a few, including the Output Hypothesis, Self-efficacy Theory, Deliberate Practice Theory, Exploratory Practice, foreign-language aptitude models, language attrition models, working memory and its role in pre-planning second language use, reading fluency definitions, Grounded Theory, communicative competence and any of its components, language proficiency, any test construct, and test validity models.

4. What are three forms theories can take?
   They can be models, hypotheses, and definitions.

5. What is an inductive approach to theory? What are three types of research using an inductive approach to theory?
   This is when we work from data, notice patterns, and then make a theory based on data and reasoning. Descriptive research, exploratory research, and Grounded Theory research are types of research associated with inductive theorizing.

6. What is a deductive approach to theory? What is the one type of research using a deducting approach to theory?
   This is when we start with an existing theory, and collect data to confirm or disconfirm the theory. Confirmatory research is associated with deductive theorizing.

7. What does HML stand for?
   High Middle Low.

8. What is grand theory or high-level theory? What is an example?
   These comprehensive theories have a broad scope and broad implications. In ordinary life, Tectonic Plate Theory is an example. In language testing, theories of test validity, communicative competence, and older conceptions of language proficiency are examples.

9. What is domain theory or middle-level theory? What is an example?
   These are theories that deal with more specific areas of concern in language learning and teaching. Examples are Self-efficacy Theory, the Output Hypothesis, and any test construct.

10. What is teacher theory or low-level theory? What is an example?
    These are personal theories that contribute to teachers' practice. An example is a teacher's thinking about what their students need and how the teacher can deal with that.

11. What kind of theory is communicative competence?
    Communicative competence is a high-level theory.

12. What is grammatical competence?
    Knowledge and ability to use the language code, including vocabulary, word formation, clause and sentence formation, pronunciation, and the writing system of the L2.

13. What is sociolinguistic competence?
    The ability to produce and interpret a language in terms of the social context, taking into account the status of the participants, the purpose of the interaction, and the expected norms and conventions for the social context.

14. What is textual competence?
    Sometimes called discourse competence, this is the ability to produce and interpret language in extended use, with both written texts and extended talk.

15. What is pragmatic competence?
    The ability to use language to accomplish social acts such as inviting or agreeing, or teaching, or expressing ones thoughts.

16. What is strategic competence?
    The ability to think about language use, and to plan, carry out, and assess accomplishment of tasks using the language.

17. What are the four features of a communicative activity or task?
    The task must allow students to actively participate, to respond to a genuine communicative need, to engage with topic areas they have some familiarity with, and to use more than one component of communicative competence (not just grammatical competence).

18. What are the four features of a communicative test?
    Test items must be task-oriented. Test items and test answers should have a communicative purpose. Test items should have some relevance to learners' experience. Answers to test items should not be overly predetermined.

DISCUSSION QUESTIONS ANSWERS

1. How would you describe your attitude toward theory? Where do you think your attitude comes from?
   It is unknown how you will answer, but you may be working with theory in other graduate classes you may be taking, or you may hear or read about theories at conferences or in journal articles. Thinking about these experiences with theories, what thoughts or feelings emerge?

2. As if to a nonapplied linguist, how would you explain the difference between the two high-level theories of language proficiency and communicative competence?
   The details of your explanation may vary, but if you focus on the difference between language knowledge without consideration of use (proficiency) versus ability to use language (communicative competence), you are probably on the right track.

3. Why would communicative competence be a high-level theory and not just a middle-level theory such as the Output Hypothesis?
   You have many other explanations, but we would emphasize that communicative competence is a model that describes what language, and language use, is. Middle-level theories describe more specific concerns, such as how teachers learn to teach language, or how students learn how to read faster and with better comprehension.

4. What are some middle-level theories about language learning or teaching that you know? Can you explain the theories to others?

If you focus on other classes you have taken, or what you have learned from conferences, books, colleagues, or other sources, you can probably name some theories. Keep notes on how complete you think your explanations are. For instance, are you able to say what a theory can be used for?

5. What is one thing you believe, as a language learner or a language teacher, about language learning? This may be an example of low theory or teacher theory.
It is unknown how you will answer, but nearly everyone can recall instances of what a teacher did that really helped us learn, or what we did as teachers that really worked well, or did not work at all. These experiences may help us find patterns that we base our theories on.

6. As a language *learner* you took tests. Were the tests communicative or do you think they focused on grammatical competence? What makes you think so?
It is unknown how you will answer, but if your teachers' tests asked you to conjugate verbs, they were focusing on grammatical competence.

7. How would our beliefs as a language *learner* affect our beliefs as a *teacher*?
You may have a variety of answers to this, but there is school of thought that theorizes that teachers end up teaching the same way they learned. This suggests that if we learned a second language focusing mainly on grammatical competence, we create in ourselves an uncommented-on tendency to teach focusing on grammar and vocabulary. There are other schools of thought that theorize that teachers are far more influenced by the need to survive during their first job. Teachers may use dialog drills not so much because that is how *they* learned, but because they have few additional ideas to keep students busy, and they sense that their employers expect them to keep students busy. Or the students may expect to be kept busy!

8. Is it always necessary that every classroom test be 100% communicative? Are there times when noncommunicative tests or subtests are appropriate? If so, what would be three to four examples?
We expect a variety of answers and ideas. One example might be a recurring error that a teacher wishes to target with a quiz. The quiz then might be used as a way to focus on the error and provide feedback to students.

APPLICATION TASK ANSWERS

1. If you are teaching, list three pedagogical practices you use in your class; if you are not teaching, list three pedagogical practices you have experienced as a student or seen used. Describe each and identify the teaching methodology (and the theory or belief) that supports these practices?

    Your practices as a teacher: Practices you experienced as a student:

    _____   _____

    _____   _____

    _____   _____

    Examples for **teacher practices** might be:

    I ask students to memorize dialogs and then they perform them to do role plays. They do this so I can correct their errors and make sure they can use the L2 appropriately in social settings.

    Students use flashcards to learn vocabulary and then they quiz each other using the flashcards. They do this because they can help each other and I think this is pairwork.

    Examples for **learner experiences** might be:

    My teacher would toss a ball to each student and we had to complete a sentence correctly that she gave us. Perhaps she thought this would help us think faster so we could say the words with the correct noun gender ending.

    We had to ask each other for information that we needed to complete a chart. Perhaps my teacher wanted us to learn how to ask questions and listen to our classmates closely.

2. Using your own test or a test your colleague would be kind enough to show you, what do you think is the test purpose? How do you know? What constructs do you see? Ask a classmate and confirm or disconfirm your impressions. How do the test items measure the constructs? Is there a TIF that might be more effective? Is the test communicative? How so?
    It is unknown what your answers will be but be sure to keep notes of the constructs you think you see in the items and your colleague's comments in response to your ideas. Make sure you compare the test items to the four characteristics of communicative tests in Chapter 4.

3. Here is part of a teacher-made test. What do you believe is the purpose of the test? What constructs do you see? Ask a classmate or

colleague and confirm or disconfirm your impressions. Is the test communicative?

This partial test may be a CRT, intended to measure students' ability to hear specific information in conversational speech. Thus the construct may be bottom up listening skills for short numbers and telephone numbers, prices, and reduced function words (I, have, etc.) used in conversations. Comparing the test constructs and TIFs to the four characteristics of communicative tests in Chapter 4, we conclude that the test items are not that task oriented. Test candidates are quite restricted in how they can answer the test items. On the other hand, the sentences seem authentic and it is possible that test candidates could have genuine responses to the items if the TIFs and test directions were different. Finally, the test items currently do not allow test candidates to provide answers that reveal more than just grammatical competence.

STUDENT WORKBOOK
CHAPTER 5

PERFORMANCE TESTS

TEST YOURSELF

Working alone or with a partner, ask and answer these questions:

1. What are the basic components of a performance test?

2. What are some decisions made using second language performance tests?

3. In this chapter, we compare NRTs, CRTs, and performance tests using 11 categories. How many can you fill in for performance tests? For an extra challenge, and to help you think of contrasts as a way to learn, can you fill in three or more for NRTs and CRTs as well? A few have been done for you (see Student Workbook Table 5.1).

4. Which two skills are considered receptive skills? Which two skills are considered productive skills? Which do performance tests seem most suited for?

5. In your own words, how would you define the term *performance test*?

6. What are the four characteristics of performance tests as defined by Norris et al. (1998) and the authors?

Table 5.1.
Student Workbook NRT, CRT, and Performance Test Comparison

	Norm-Referenced Tests	Criterion-Referenced Tests	Performance Tests
Also known as:	Standardized tests, proficiency tests		
A metaphor is:		Students knowing	
Functions to:			
Used for:		Diagnosis and achievement	
Preferred by:			
Written by:			
Getting and using one:			
A good item is:			
Aim for:	High percentile scores		
Content:			
Reliability:			

7. What are ways a performance test can be connected to the course curriculum?

8. What is the *real world* in the performance test model? What does the real world have to do with a performance test?

9. Why might some performance tests be only general purpose, and thus less connected to the real world?

10. What are performance test criteria based on?

11. What is the difference between a *holistic scale* and an *analytic scale*?

12. What are the four types of performance test tasks?

13. What are examples of *stakeholders*? What are some answers we should provide them?

14. What does it mean to *pilot* a test?

15. What is a *scale*?

16. How do performance tests produce a score?

DISCUSSION QUESTIONS

1. Have you participated in a performance test as a learner? Describe it. What was the test score used for? Looking back, what was an advantage of the test? What was a disadvantage?

2. In writing and/or using a performance test, what are some practical problems you would anticipate?

3. In giving a performance test, what would you hope to achieve? What would be the benefits?

4. What sources can you think of, right at this moment, that you could use to decide a task and criteria to use? How would you obtain this source?

5. Can a TREE simply use task and criteria they find in a book or on the internet? What could a TREE do to ensure the task and criteria fit their situation?

6. Many programs elect to use a general purpose performance test using an interview format with preset criteria. What would be an advantage of using such a test? What would be a disadvantage?

7. We highlight ten points to write a performance test. If you plan to give multiple, smaller, low-stakes performance tests, are there any steps you can skip to save time?

8. What are some ways you can compensate colleagues for being raters on your test? Does the compensation have to be cash?

APPLICATION TASKS

1. If you are currently teaching, select a chapter from the textbook you are using. Choose two communicative activities or tasks from the chapter. Alternatively, select two communicative tasks you commonly do in class, such as role plays, or learners doing pair work to teach each other new vocabulary from a text, or weekly e-mails learners send to pen pals. Write up the tasks for two different performance tests, and write the purposes of the tests. Show your tasks and your stated purposes to classmates and colleagues. Do they think the tasks for the tests match your purposes?

2. Explain the connection between the two tasks you selected for #1 and the real world in which the student might be expected to operate. In other words, how do the tasks reflect what your students might be expected to do? How would you find out more about learners' real-world needs?

3. Search and find online video-recorded second language speaking samples for the purpose of exploring what your learners need to use their second language for. Describe the setting and purpose for the video speakers' talk. Make a list of tasks that you observe the learners doing, such as answering questions, giving a short speech, or ordering food. Write a short list of performance test tasks that might capture similar skills to what the speakers are doing on the video. Finally, write a short of list of criteria that you might use to judge the video speakers' talk.

   Here are some examples of Japanese-language speech contests. Speech contests are a common feature of foreign language education in Japan.

   Japanese-language speech contest in Japan (video of one contestant): https://www.youtube.com/watch?v=7pakfqh-XUI

   Japanese-language speech contest in Kuala Lumpur (video of one contestant): https://www.youtube.com/watch?v=DQ_zvRH7fJs

4. Find the syllabus for a second language course. Many are available online and can be found with some judicious search terms. Find the course objectives. If a performance test were used in the course, what criteria should be used that would match the course objec-

tives? Make a list of possible criteria, and then connect the criteria to high-, middle-, and/or low-level theories. Does the syllabus mention a performance test? Are criteria already listed in the syllabus? If so, compare them to the criteria *you* decided on.

5. Find some actual writing samples of second language learners online or see whether you can collect some locally, *ensuring the students' names are erased*. Find out what task or prompt that the learners responded to, and what level the learners are supposed to be. Also find criteria and a scale for the writing task. If there is no scale, write a scale that is relevant to the criteria. Score the writing samples and write your impressions and feedback on the test task and the criteria. Plan and give an oral report about a pilot performance test you have "given" using the writing samples. Include specific ideas on how to revise the test task and the criteria.

Sample sources: We offer some online sources that were located using various search terms. We note that due to the dynamic nature of the internet, some of these links will not work. If you find additional links not listed here, share them with your classmates and colleagues!

Writing samples from K-12 ESL learners: http://www.learnalberta.ca/content/eslapb/writing_samples.html

Sample writing and speaking tasks, and writing and speaking criteria and scales: http://www.nus.edu.sg/celc/research/books/4th%20Symposium%20proceedings/19%29.%20Radhikda%20De%20Silva.pdf

Example writing task prompts for German learners: http://www.goethe.de/lrn/pro/sd1/data/schreiben.htm

Sample tasks and criteria with scales for writing and speaking, and abbreviated writing samples in German: http://carla.umn.edu/assessment/MLPA/pdfs/Speaking_Writing_Tasks_Guide.pdf

Sample tasks from a French writing test (p. 13): http://www.nysedregents.org/loteslp/french/exam_609.pdf

Sample criteria and scales for the French writing test listed above: http://www.nysedregents.org/loteslp/french/slp-french-rg-610p.pdf

Sample tasks and criteria for writing in Japanese (pp. 10–14): http://www.vcaa.vic.edu.au/Documents/exams/japanese2nd/2005japslsamp.pdf

TEST YOURSELF ANSWERS

1. What are the basic components of a performance test?
   Some kind of activity or task for the test candidates to do, criteria by which to judge the performances, and some of scale applied to the criteria.

2. What are some decisions made using the results of second language performance tests?
   We name many, but we start off with: (a) whether a graduate student speaks English well enough to teach university-level classes in English-speaking university, and (b) whether healthcare workers have good enough Japanese to work in hospitals or elder care facilities.

3. In this chapter, we compare NRTs, CRTs, and performance tests using 11 categories. How many can you fill in for performance tests? For an extra challenge, and to help you think of contrasts as a way to learn, can you fill in three or more for NRTs and CRTs as well? A few have been done for you (see Workbook Table 5.2).

Table 5.2.
Student Workbook NRT, CRT, and Performance Test Comparison Answers

	Norm-Referenced Tests	*Criterion-Referenced Tests*	*Performance Tests*
Also known as:	Standardized tests, proficiency tests	Teacher-made tests, class quizzes, mid-term exams, final exams	Role-plays, simulations, class presentations, final projects, written reports
A metaphor is:	Comparing students	Students knowing	Students doing
Functions to:	Compare students to a well-defined norming group	Compare students to well-defined course objectives	Rate students on criteria of interest
Used for:	Admission and placement	Diagnosis and achievement	Diagnosis and achievement

(Table continues on next page)

Table 5.2.
Test Comparison Answers (Continued)

	Norm-Referenced Tests	Criterion-Referenced Tests	Performance Tests
Preferred by:	Administrators	Classroom teachers	Classroom teachers and students
Written by:	Testing professionals	Classroom teachers	Classroom teachers and program directors
Getting and using one:	Easy to buy, difficult to make, easy to score	Hard to buy, somewhat difficult to make, often easy to score	Easy to make, hard to score
A good item is:	One that lower-ability students get wrong and higher ability students get right	One that most of the students initially get wrong and then later get right	A task and criteria that capture the construct
Aim for:	High percentile scores	High scores	High ratings on criteria
Content:	Is the same for all test takers	Depends on the theoretical construct and course content	Varies with the task
Reliability:	Assumes normal distribution	May or may not result in normal distribution	Is obtained by inter rater reliability and rater training

4. Which two skills are considered receptive skills? Which two skills are considered productive skills? Which do performance tests seem most suited for?
   Listening and reading are termed receptive skills, and speaking and writing are termed productive skills. Intuitively, performance tests are well suited for speaking and writing.

5. In your own words, how would you define the term *performance test*?
   It is a test in which learners demonstrate their ability to use the second language while engaging in a task that resembles a likely future assignment or need.

6. What are the four characteristics of performance tests as defined by Norris et al. (1998) and the authors?
   Test candidates are engaged in the performance of a task; test candidates are engaged in authentic tasks, meaning that the task is as close

as possible to a real-life task; test candidates' performance of a task are judged by raters; and test candidates have some input into the task or some component of the task, meaning that performance tests can accommodate some degree of learner decision making on how to address the task.

7. What are ways a performance test can be connected to the course curriculum?

    A performance test can be connected to the curriculum by listing and then choosing test tasks that are supported by the course curriculum. In other words, does the curriculum support learners' ability to do well on the test? Test criteria and their scales can also be connected to the curriculum by focusing on aspects of learners' performances that are relevant to the course outcomes. One way to do a reality check is to show the course outcomes, and the tasks and criteria, to colleagues or classmates. You can ask: "Do you think the outcomes can support learners doing this test task?" "Do these criteria seem relevant to the course?"

8. What is the *real world* in the performance test model? What does the real world have to do with a performance test?

    The *real world* means the language use situations learners will likely encounter, such as being a healthcare worker or a successful high school student. Ideally, thinking about the real world will assist TREEs to make lists of possible tasks to use in performance tests.

9. Why might some performance tests be only general purpose and perhaps less connected to the real world?

    Students in some courses may have diverse future language use needs, and it may not be possible for TREEs to construct separate tasks for each learner. It may be difficult for teachers to know the entire domain of future language use needs for learners, even though they should make efforts to find out.

10. What are performance test criteria based on?

    Performance test criteria are based on high-, middle-, and sometimes low-level theories. What is important is that the theory and criteria have a clear connection.

11. What is the difference between a *holistic scale* and an *analytic scale*?

    A holistic scale is a single scale. Each point on the scale has a lengthy description of learners' abilities at that level, which is made up of multiple criteria. An analytic scale is multiple scales, each of which makes up a test criterion. Descriptions for each point of the scale are short.

TREEs may use a holistic scale when they have 20 or more performances to score or when there is no need for diagnostic feedback to learners. Analytic scales provide specific diagnostic feedback as each scale describes one aspect of a performance to be scored.

12. What are the four types of performance test tasks?
    Direct assessment (an observation actually done in a workplace); work sample (an observation done in an authentic but controlled setting, such as working as a cashier with a supervisor, there to help); simulation (doing a task that is similar to real life, such as a role play); and pedagogical work (doing an ordinary communicative task in a classroom, such as an opinion gap activity or giving directions to locate a place on a map).

13. What are examples of *stakeholders*? What are some answers we should provide them?
    Examples could be teachers, administrators, students, parents or sponsors of students, or colleagues. We should be able to provide a succinct description of what the performance test is supposed to measure, who is test is designed for, and what decisions a performance test can be used for. The TREE/test writer should clearly describe the limitations of a performance test, particularly if it is a high stakes test.

14. What does it mean to *pilot* a test?
    This means to give the test as a trial run in similar conditions to which the actual test would be given. The pilot is done to get feedback from individuals taking the test, and from raters. The purpose of the pilot is to guide revisions to the test (the task, and criteria and scales) and the test procedure (how much time is allowed, etc.).

15. What is a *scale*?
    A scale is a unit of measurement. In the context of performance tests, scales are applied to criteria that have been selected for the test. Some scales are numbered (1 = low ability, 2 = middle ability, etc.) and some rely on brief titles, such as "task not achieved," "some elements of task achieved," and "task achieved." Each level on the scale has a criterion-relevant description, and it is on the basis of the description, and the input of stakeholders, that cut points are made.

16. How do performance tests produce a score?
    Raters observe a performance and use the criteria and the scales applied to them to produce a numerical score. Some performance tests result in written, qualitative data, but usually numerical data are used

to pass or fail learners, or to assign grades. If a holistic scale is used then one number is produced. If an analytic scale is used, the numbers on each scale are often added up to a total, or are averaged to create a score.

DISCUSSION QUESTIONS ANSWERS

1. Have you participated in a performance test as a learner? Describe it. What was the test score used for? Looking back, what was an advantage of the test? What was a disadvantage?
   Take some time to think about this question, particularly the part about being able to describe the test. It may have been low stakes, such as a written assignment in a class. This may be a good time to consider your students as being good sources of feedback.

2. In writing and/or using a performance test, what are some practical problems you would anticipate?
   Time is likely the biggest concern. Performance tests take time to write, and more-than-anticipated time to administer and score. This is likely to be most evident for spoken tests. Some language teachers elect to administer interview tests and other oral tests over a two or three day period with five or six candidates at a time. On the other hand, if the TREE has decided on criteria and a scale, and learns to use it efficiently, scoring may become the shortest part of a performance test administration. At any rate, keep a list of answers you come up with for this question, and find ways to solve them, or focus on explaining the benefits despite the practical problems.

3. In giving a performance test, what would you hope to achieve? What would be the benefits?
   Many TREEs like the idea of directly observing the abilities of learners while using the language. Results on a performance test, particularly as diagnosis, gives teachers good ideas what learners still need to work on so they can use the second language in the real world. Also consult the "advantages" section of Chapter 5. See if you can add one or two more items to the list.

4. What sources can you think of, right at this moment, that you could use to decide a task and criteria to use? How would you obtain this source?
   There is, of course, Textbook Table 5.2. Some second language textbooks have performance tests described, and some testing books have sample tasks and criteria. There are also many internet sources. If your

school library does not already do have a document retrieval service, urge them to subscribe to one, and enlist their help in finding journal articles and book chapters.

5. Can a TREE simply use task and criteria they find in a book or on the internet? What could a TREE do to ensure the task and criteria fit their situation?
A needs analysis will help teachers find the domain of real world tasks learners will need to do using the second language. The TREE will need to compare his or her understanding of needed tasks, based on evidence, to the task suggested by the performance test from a book or another source. The teacher will also need to consider whether his or her course prepares the learners to succeed at the task. Criteria are selected for their relevance to the high-, middle-, and low-level theories the teacher uses to teach, which we hope are connected to communicative competence. Also, the criteria should be relevant to the course curriculum. If speaking fluency is not addressed in a course, there is no point in using a speaking fluency criterion to judge students' presentations or teaching simulations. Finally, some criteria have no practical relationship to the testing procedure. If learners use word processors to write their essays, then there is no point to judging learners' neatness, writing by hand.

6. Many programs elect to use a general purpose performance test using an interview format with pre-set criteria. What would be an advantage of using such a test? What would be a disadvantage?
If a program has the money to bring official examiners for the test to the school, wonderful. On the one hand, students will get a score that they can use to compare themselves to other students in other schools who have taken the same test. If the test is well known and respected, the scores can be used to get into study abroad programs or into college. On the other hand, doing a spoken interview may be not relevant to other tasks learners may wish to do in the second language, such as shopping, setting up an oil rig, taking care of the elderly, writing an application for summer study, and getting along with others in an office situation.

7. We highlight 10 points to write a performance test. If you plan to give multiple, smaller, low-stakes performance tests, are there any steps you can skip to save time?
Probably not. All 10 points all need more, or less, attention, as the teacher can give them. But Davis and Kondo Brown (2012) advocate test criteria and scales that do not have to be specific to a particular

test task. Rather, the criteria are related to the course curriculum. Thus, once a set of writing task criteria and scales are established, they can be used for any writing task the TREE decides to give. De Silva (2014) does something similar for both speaking tasks and writing tasks.

8. What are some ways you can compensate colleagues for being raters on your test? Does the compensation have to be cash?
You can offer them dinner, rating services on their performance tests, or a letter of commendation to their supervisor.

APPLICATION TASKS ANSWERS

1. If you are currently teaching, select a chapter from the textbook you are using. Choose two communicative activities or tasks from the chapter. Alternatively, select two communicative tasks you commonly do in class, such as role plays, or learners doing pair work to teach each other new vocabulary from a text, or weekly e-mails learners send to pen pals. Write up the tasks for two different performance tests, and write the purpose of the tests. Show your tasks and your stated purposes to classmates and colleagues. Do they think the tasks for the tests match your purpose?
Your tasks should be stated as test directions that learners will respond to. This means there needs to be enough detail so that learners know what to do (and so colleagues know what learners need to do). One way to "test" the task directions is to read it to one or two students and ask them how they would respond. Your statements of purpose for the two tests need to be at the level of detail of test specifications, such as "This test is designed to gauge learners' ability to ask questions and get information about different trains he or she can catch to Milan, including their times, costs, and services provided on the train."

2. Explain the connection between the two tasks you selected for #1 and the real world in which the student might be expected to operate. In other words, how do the tasks reflect what your students might be expected to do? How would you find out more about learners' real world needs?
Here is a table with some suggestions for the first part of the task: Suggestions for finding out more about learners' real world needs include asking learners in a questionnaire, interviewing your learners, finding an article from the second language field that reports on a needs analysis, or interviewing colleagues and supervisors (see Student Workbook Table 5.3).

Table 5.3.
Student Workbook Performance Test Tasks and Real World Tasks

Possible Classroom Performance Test Tasks	How Related to Future Real-World Tasks
Casual conversation role plays	Speak to a friend in the second language country
Writing in a specific genre (description, comparison, etc.)	Writing an academic research paper
Formal interviews face to face or on Skype, etc.	Job interview
Presentation	Approach to teach using the second language
Ordering food in a restaurant	Visiting the second language country
Asking for directions	Visiting the second language country
Talking about the weather	Visiting the second language country
Writing a short book review in the second language	Participating in an online book club in the second language country
Writing a summary of a recorded talk in the second language	Summarizing notes from a class and preparing for a test in history, communication, etc.

3. Search and find online video-recorded, real-world second language speaking samples for the purpose of exploring what your learners need to use their second language for. Describe the setting and purpose for the video speakers' talk. Make a list of tasks that you observe the learners doing, such as answering questions, giving a short speech, or ordering food. Write a short list of performance test tasks that might capture similar skills to what the speakers are doing on the video. Finally, write a short of list of criteria that you might use to judge the video speakers' talk.

   It is unknown what you will find, but at minimum you need to address the points of application task #1, including describing the setting and purpose for the speakers' talk, etc. Consider making a table like the one for application task #2, including a column for possible criteria to use to judge the tasks based on real-world needs observed in the video recordings.

4. Find the syllabus for a second language course. Many are available online and can be found with some judicious search terms. Find the course objectives. If a performance test were used in the course, what criteria should be used, that would match the course objec-

tives? Make a list of possible criteria, and then connect the criteria to high-, middle-, and/or low-level theories. Does the syllabus mention a performance test? Are criteria already listed in the syllabus? If so, compare them to the criteria *you* decided on.

It is unknown what you will find. One syllabus was found using the search term *Cornell University Russian syllabus*: http://russian.cornell.edu/index.cfm?MainFrameURL=description&Section=currentclasses&CourseID=RUSSA1104-101&LinkID=RUSSA1104-101

We can see the course objectives, which include "fluency, accuracy and authentic flair of speech by practicing conversation in Russian on a variety of topics" and "improve Russian pronunciation." You may wish to make a table for the objectives you find on a course syllabus and for each one name which high-level theory the course objective seems to originate from. Read the syllabus carefully and do not assume that just because a course focuses on conversation, that the course designer focuses on aspects of communicative competence other than grammatical competence. Ability to use correct syntax would thus require a criterion only about syntax, not about communicative ability overall. You should end up with a list of at least five criteria, along with the high-, middle-, and low-level theories you believe support them.

5. Find some actual writing samples of second language learners online or see whether you can collect some locally, *ensuring the students' names are erased*. Find out what task or prompt that the learners responded to and what level the learners are supposed to be. Also find criteria and a scale for the writing task. If there is no scale, write a scale that is relevant to the criteria. Score the writing samples and write your impressions and feedback on the test task and the criteria. Plan and give an oral report about a pilot performance test you have "given" using the writing samples. Include specific ideas on how to revise the test task and the criteria.

Your report should amount to a pilot test report that you can use to argue for test validity of your performance test. This means revealing all of the "warts" and imperfections of the test, but, more important, giving specific plans on how to revise the test.

STUDENT WORKBOOK
CHAPTER 6

DESCRIPTIVE STATISTICS

TEST YOURSELF

Working alone or with a study partner, ask and answer these questions:

1. What are the four scales discussed in this chapter?

2. What is one characteristic of each scale?

3. Give a practical example of each scale.

4. Explain what "test range" is.

5. Many teachers would arrange students' test scores alphabetically by students' names. What would be the benefit of ordering students' scores from highest to lowest?

6. What is the difference between central tendency and dispersion?

7. What are the elements of a histogram?

8. What is the relationship between a histogram and a distribution?

9. What is the difference between the mean and the mode?

10. Explain standard deviation in your own words. Why would it be useful to understand a distribution?

11. What is the difference between skewness and kurtosis?

12. What are two properties of a normal distribution?

13. What are two reasons (out of many) a distribution might not be normal?

14. At minimum, what information should you report when using or presenting on a test?

DISCUSSION QUESTIONS

1. For many readers, this may be the first contact with statistics. Nonetheless, what knowledge, intuitions, or experience from before reading this book seem applicable to this chapter's content? What about scales, distributions, and descriptive statistics makes sense to you? What remains unclear to you?

2. The data in Textbook Table 6.2 and Textbook Figure 6.1 were discussed in terms of the distribution resulting from a norm-referenced test and a criterion-referenced test. If you used this test and got the distribution shown in Figure 6.1, would you be happy if this were a norm-referenced test? Why? Why not? Would you have any problem with using this distribution to make admissions decisions to a program?

3. This builds on discussion question #2. If you used this test and got the distribution shown in Student Workbook Figure 6.1, would you be happy if this were a criterion-referenced test given as a posttest? Why or why not? Would you have any problem with using this distribution to assign a final grade to students?

4. What would account for outliers? What could cause a person to be an outlier? Could we simply take an outlier out of the data set and then use the now-more-normal distribution for further statistical analysis? What would be the positive or negative points of removing outliers from the data set?

APPLICATION TASKS

1. Here are some test scores on a 25-item test. How many of the following descriptive statistics can you calculate? (See Student Workbook Table 6.1).

Table 6.1.
Application Task #1 Dataset

Student	Score
1	14
2	12
3	15
4	14
5	12
6	11
7	9
8	7
9	12
10	11
11	24
12	19
13	13
14	12
15	10
16	9
17	11
18	12
19	2

n	
Test score range (K)	
Mean	
Median	
Mode	
Min/max	
Standard Deviation	
Skewness	
Standard Error of Skewness (optional)	

Fisher's Skewness Coefficient (optional)	
Kurtosis	
Standard Error of Kurtosis (optional)	
Fisher's Kurtosis Coefficient (optional)	

2. Draw a histogram for the data set in application task #1 (see Student Workbook Figure 6.1).

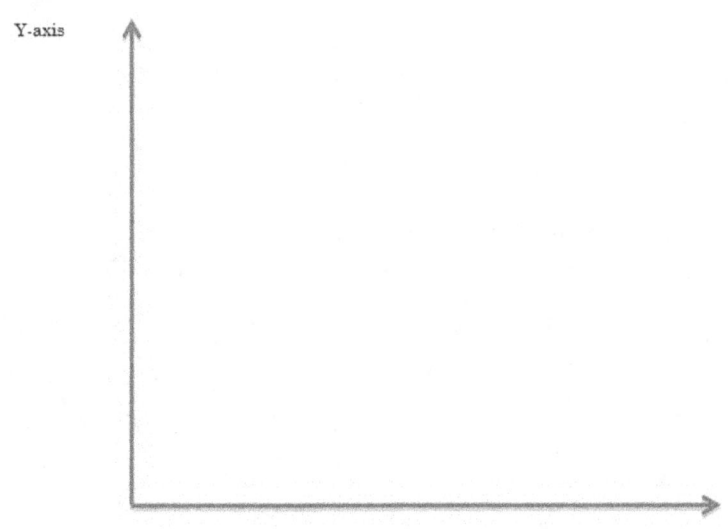

Figure 6.1. Histogram for Student Workbook Table 6.1 dataset.

3. Select three strategies or arguments to determine the degree to which the scores from application task #1 are normally distributed.

Strategy one: _____

Write your argument here based on the data set. If you are doing calculations, show them here.

Strategy two: _____

Write your argument here based on the data set. If you are doing calculations, show them here.

Strategy three: _____

Write your argument here based on the dataset. If you are doing calculations, show them here.

4. What does the distribution from application task #1 tell you if:

   a. The test is intended as a norm-referenced test?
   b. The test is intended as the pretest for a criterion-referenced test?
   c. The test is intended as the posttest for a criterion-referenced test?

TEST YOURSELF ANSWERS

1. What are the four scales discussed in this chapter?
   Nominal, ordinal, interval, and ratio.

2. What is one characteristic of each scale?
   Nominal scales are sets of categories and have no implicit order. Ordinal scales have an implicit order but the distance between the points on the scale is unknown. Interval scales have an order and there is approximately the same distance between the points on the scale. Ratio scales have a true zero point.

3. Give a practical example of each scale. Answers will vary, but here are examples.
   Nominal scale: Learners who have done home stay abroad and those who have not.
   Ordinal scale: Learners' class ranking.
   Interval scale: Ratings of learners on a five point holistic scale for a performance test.
   Ratio scale: Length of time learner has studied language X.

4. Explain what "test range" is.
   This is the total possible score learners can get on a test—in other words, from the lowest possible score on a test to the highest possible score.

5. Many teachers would arrange students' test scores alphabetically by students' names. What, then, would be the benefit of ordering students' scores from highest to lowest?

Ordering learners' scores from highest to lowest helps us see patterns in the distribution more clearly.

6. What is the difference between central tendency and dispersion?
Central tendency is how scores in a distribution are similar, or how they group together.
Dispersion is how scores are spread out in a distribution, and how widely they vary.

7. What are the elements of a histogram?
There is a horizontal axis showing test scores from 0 to the maximum score (test range), and a vertical axis showing frequency of learners getting a particular score. Frequencies may be shown as a vertical bar or a series of points. The higher the bar or points, the more learners got a particular score on a test.

8. What is the relationship between a histogram and a distribution?
Histograms are a way of visualizing a distribution. Thus, histograms are a visual representation of a distribution. If a histogram shows a peak in the middle of the x-axis with equal slopes on both the left and the right, the distribution may be normal. If a histogram has a very high peak either to the right or the left of the middle of the x-axis, then the distribution may not be normal. It means that learners as a group either found the test easy or difficult. If a histogram has a very low peak, or no peak, it may mean the distribution is not normal. It may mean that learners did not interact with the test as a group, and that, according to the test, learners' knowledge varies widely.

9. What is the difference between the mean and the mode?
The mean is a mathematical average of all scores in a data set. The mode is the most common score in the data set. The mean is sensitive to outliers, while the mode is less sensitive to outliers.

10. Explain standard deviation in your own words. Why would it be useful to understand a distribution?
Answers may vary. They should contain some element like, "SD is the average distance from learners from the mean of a test." Answers may also include the idea that the formula for SD needs to change according to n size.

11. What is the difference between skewness and kurtosis?
Skewness is a measure of dispersion and kurtosis is a measure of central tendency. Skewness shows whether learners responded as a

group to a test, and kurtosis shows how widely learners varied in their test scores.

12. What are two properties of a normal distribution?
    There are multiple answers to this, but two would be: There is a peak in the middle of the test range: 50% of the learners are to the left of the mean, and 50% are to the right of the mean. Can you think of other answers?

13. What are two reasons (out of many) a distribution might not be normal?
    There are multiple answers to this, but two would be: The test is easy or difficult in relation to the learners. There may be outliers in the dataset. Can you think of additional answers?

14. At minimum, what information should you report when using or presenting on a test?
    Show a histogram. Calculate descriptive statistics. Calculate standard error of skewness and standard error of kurtosis.

DISCUSSION QUESTIONS ANSWERS

1. For many readers, this may be the first contact with statistics. Nonetheless, what knowledge, intuitions, or experience from before reading this book seem applicable to this chapter's content? What about scales, distributions, and descriptive statistics makes sense to you? What remains unclear to you?
   Answers will vary, of course. Many find scales initially hard to grasp because it is not clear how they are related to analyzing a test—interval scales are the never-discussed default and the most familiar in our folk knowledge of testing, and perhaps then the hardest to objectify. The main point is to be able to state what you do not understand and seek answers.

2. The data in Textbook Table 6.2 and Textbook Figure 6.1 were discussed in terms of the distribution resulting from a norm-referenced test and a criterion-referenced test. If you used this test and got the distribution shown in Textbook Figure 6.1, would you be happy if this were a norm-referenced test? Why? Why not? Would you have any problem with using this distribution to make admissions decisions to a program?
   This distribution would probably result from a norm-referenced test given to a smaller group of learners. The distribution is somewhat

non-normal, with a large *SD* and a negative skew. There are only 1½ *SD*s to the right of the mean. Still, the standard error of skewness and kurtosis are within the convention bounds of normal, and the Fisher's coefficients are not significant. There are no outliers, strictly speaking. Some TREEs might find it easy and defensible to use the histogram (Figure 6.1) to admit learners who got scores of 84 and more, or 64 and up.

3. This builds on discussion question #2. If you used this test and got the distribution shown in Textbook Figure 6.1, would you be happy if this were a criterion-referenced test given as a posttest? Why or why not? Would you have any problem with using this distribution to assign a final grade to students?
This distribution would make most TREEs unhappy if this were a post-test. Kurtosis is somewhat negative, and Figure 6.1 confirms that some learners are widely spread out on the x-axis. While many learners did relative well on the test, quite a few learners still seem to know 60% or less of the content captured in the test. It may mean the test was not well designed. Or it may mean that the instruction did not match the test. Using traditional, rarely-discussed folk thinking about human ability, some teachers may think the distribution was fine for awarding grades of A, B, C, etc. (see Chapters 3, 4, and 10 for alternative models). Other test users would find the distribution too spread out to awarding grades of "pass" and "fail."

4. What would account for outliers? What could cause a person to be an outlier? Could we simply take an outlier out of the data set and then use the now-more-normal distribution for further statistical analysis? What would be the positive or negative points of removing outliers from the data set?
Learners may be outliers with low scores because they did not attend class, or because they have visual or hearing disabilities or some other disability that may not be apparent. Learners may also be outliers because they were placed into a class incorrectly from the beginning. Examples of this might be learners who lived in the country where the second language is used, or heritage second language learners. Other examples might be learners who simply have trouble retaining sounds or words and who need extra help.

In removing outliers from a dataset, a good deal of thought and transparency is needed. On the one hand, an outlier is part of the naturally occurring test group. Pett (1997) tells us that outliers "provide information about the types of cases that may not fit a particular hypothesized model." This means that perhaps we have not taken into account that some learners who score low need more instruction, or different type of instruction, than we thought, for example. On the other hand, outliers strongly affect distributions and descriptive statistics. We suggest keeping an outlier in a data set. If an outlier or outliers are taken out of a data set, TREEs need to account for why this was done.

APPLICATION TASK ANSWERS

1. Here are some test scores on a 25-item test. How many of the following descriptive statistics can you calculate?

   Reordered from highest to lower scores, the data set now appears as shown in Table 6.2 in the Student Workbook.

   Table 6.2.
   Application Task #1 Dataset

Student	Score
11	24
12	19
3	15
1	14
4	14
13	13
2	12
5	12
9	12
14	12
18	12
6	11
10	11
17	11
15	10
7	9
16	9
8	7
19	2

n	19
Test score range (*K*)	25
Mean	12.05
Median	12
Mode	12
Min/max	2/24
Standard Deviation	4.48 (using the sample population formula)
Skewness	.60
Standard Error of Skewness (optional)	Using Brown's formula (Appendix C) .56
	Using alternate formula (Appendix C) .52
Fisher's Skewness Coefficient (optional)	Using Brown's formula for standard error of skewness 1.07
	Using alternate formula for standard error of skewness 1.15
Kurtosis	2.96
Standard Error of Kurtosis (optional)	Using Brown's formula (Appendix C) 1.09
	Using alternate formula with alternate formula for standard error of skewness 1.01
Fisher's Kurtosis Coefficient (optional)	Using estimation of standard error of kurtosis using Brown's formula (Appendix C) 2.72
	Using estimation of standard error of kurtosis using alternate formula (Appendix C) 2.93

2. Draw a histogram for the data set in application task #1 (Figure 6.2).

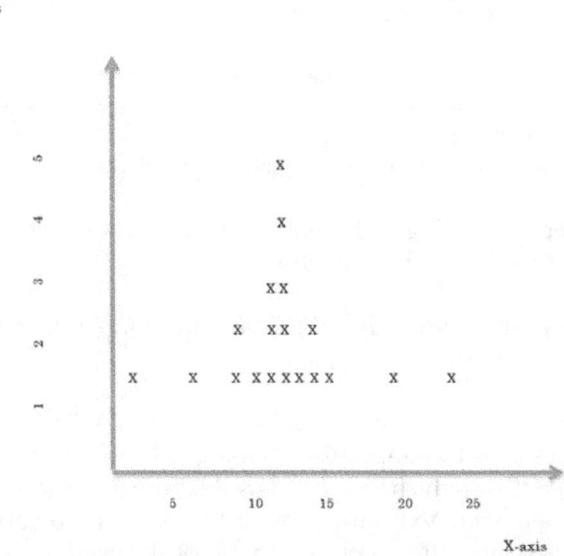

Figure 6.2. Histgram for Student Workbook Table 6.2 dataset.

3. Select three strategies, or arguments, to determine the degree to which the scores from application task #1 are normally distributed.

Strategy 1: Present a histogram. Look at the histogram and ask others to comment.

Write your argument here based on the data set. If you are doing calculations, show them here.

Does the histogram appear to have a peak around the middle of the x-axis? Do the slopes of the distribution fall away in a way that looks symmetrical? On one hand, there is a peak generally in the middle of the x-axis and there appear to be roughly equal slopes both to the left and the right of the highest peak. On the other hand, the peak appears very high in relation to the rest of the distribution. However, this distribution may be in the bounds of normal. More analysis is needed. This histogram was shown to two colleagues. One thought the distribution looked normal but the other did not. This concurs with my judgment that the distribution needs more analysis.

Strategy 2: Look at the descriptive statistics.

Write your argument here based on the data set. If you are doing calculations, show them here.

The mean, median, and mode are very close (12.05, 12, 12). The skewness index is less than 2 (.60). But the kurtosis index is greater than 2 (2.96), which accounts for the high peak. This distribution may not be in the bounds of normal. More analysis is needed.

Strategy 3: Adding and subtracting 3 *SD*s from the mean to see if the distribution is symmetrical.

Write your argument here based on the data set. If you are doing calculations, show them here.

The mean is 12.05 and the *SD* is 4.48. 12.05 − 4.48 − 4.48 − 4.48 = −1.39, which is impossible, below 0. 12.04 + 4.48 + 4.48 + 4.48 = 25.48, which is also impossible with a test score range of 25. There seem to be just under 3 *SD*s on each side of the mean, which are nonetheless pretty symmetrical. Given the previous two analyses, with the exception of the high kurtosis, this distribution may be within the bounds of normal. Perhaps both parametric and nonparametric statistics can be used.

Other strategies include: Estimating standard error of skewness and kurtosis, calculating Fisher's coefficients of skewness and kurtosis, and checking for outliers using z-scores.

4. What does the distribution from application task #1 tell you if:

   a. The test is intended as a norm-referenced test?
      Students are spread out over a score continuum, and this would be expected with an NRT. However, for an NRT, 25 items is not very much. There is a large peak in the middle with the vast bulk of learners getting scores in the middle with actually few learners getting high or low scores. In a normal distribution, we would expect 11.44% of learners to be between 2 and 3 *SD*s above or below the mean. But only 1 learner, or 5% of the distribution, got a score of 2, which is between 2 and 3 *SD*s below the mean. The test is not as useful as it could be to discriminate between learners with lower ability, or between learners in a higher ability group. The data suggest that this test, if used as an NRT for admissions or placement, should be increased with length, with more easy and more difficult items.

b. The test is intended as the pretest for a criterion-referenced test? Quite a few learners got scores in the middle but few in the upper test score range. This finding suggests that the majority of learners do not yet "have" at least some of the content that is tested. This may be acceptable as a pretest to proceed with the course because it appears learners have room to improve. Because so many learners got the same scores (mode = 12), test security should be checked. Were these learners sitting together? Alternatively, did they come from similar educational backgrounds?

c. The test is intended as the posttest for a criterion-referenced test? This distribution leaves something to be desired for a posttest. On the one hand, learners converged strongly in the middle, suggesting that instruction is having some effect. Learners' answers and abilities are very similar. One the other hand, many learners are getting less than half of the items correct. The content may be harder than previously thought, or some content has not gotten the coverage it needs, or the test did not cover all of the course content equally. Again, check test security. Have the test been used with previous courses? Were similarly scoring learners sitting together?

STUDENT WORKBOOK
CHAPTER 7

CORRELATION

TEST YOURSELF

Working alone or with a study partner, ask and answer these questions:

1. What are at least two ways you can use correlation in testing?

2. What is positive correlation? What would a positive correlation coefficient look like?

3. What is negative correlation? What would a negative correlation coefficient look like?

4. Are negative correlations bad? Why or why not?

5. What are the names of three correlation procedures?

6. Which correlations are parametric? In what situations would you use them?

7. Which correlation is nonparametric? In what situation would you use it?

8. What is an assumption? Why are they important?

9. What is causality? What is the relevance of the idea of causality to correlation?

10. What is effect size?

11. Name the assumptions of Pearson product-moment correlation.

12. Describe the two kinds of variables needed to use point-biserial correlation.

13. In what circumstances would you use Spearman rank-order correlation?

14. How do you get the kind of scales needed for Spearman rank-order correlation?

15. What are two measures that tell us the strength of a correlation?

16. What is a *P*-value and what is it used for?

DISCUSSION QUESTIONS

1. Correlation is a commonly used statistical procedure in testing and research. What kind of experience have you had using correlation? Or, have you read reports than mention using it? What connections can you make between your previous experience and this chapter?

2. List five pairs of variables you would like to correlate. Use Student Workbook Table 7.1, and share your answers with a classmate. Write down their feedback.

3. The text lists assumptions for each of the three correlations. What are the assumptions the three correlations have in common? Are any of the assumptions unique to one or two of the correlations? Which of these assumptions do you feel most confident exploring? Which of these assumptions do you feel least confident exploring?

4. In second and foreign language testing, we often have small sample sizes and nonnormal distributions. Does it necessarily follow that we have to use a nonparametric correlation? How should we decide?

Table 7.1.
Student Workbook Correlation Variable Description Assignment

Variable Pairs	Scale	Positive or Negative Correlation Expected or Not Sure	Classmate's Feedback
Correlation #1			
Variable X:	Variable X:		
Variable Y:	Variable Y:		
Correlation #2			
Variable X:	Variable X:		
Variable Y:	Variable Y:		
Correlation #3			
Variable X:	Variable X:		
Variable Y:	Variable Y:		
Correlation #4			
Variable X:	Variable X:		
Variable Y:	Variable Y:		
Correlation #5			
Variable X:	Variable X:		
Variable Y:	Variable Y:		

5. This question builds on discussion question #2. Do you think that there may be a third variable Z that would affect any of the X and Y variables you would like to correlate?

6. As if to a colleague or a supervisor, explain what *P*-values should and should not be used for.

7. What points about correlation remain unclear to you? Write them here and ask about them during class or office hours, or through your own reading.

8. What points about correlation do you feel clear about, that you can explain or use with confidence? Consider offering to teach it to your classmates, or review it with them using your own data.

APPLICATION TASKS

1. Retrieve one of the following articles using correlation. Many online articles become unavailable due to the dynamic nature of the internet. You should learn how to use the document retrieval capabilities of academic libraries near you. Many online articles that have become unavailable may still be available through your library document retrieval system. Further, do not avoid an article just because the date makes it seem "old." Inquiry such as that done by Currall and Kirk (1986) and Cziko (1982), for example, is never dated.

Currall, S., & Kirk, R. (1986). Predicting success in intensive foreign language courses. *The Modern Language Journal, 70*(2), 107–113.
Cziko, G. (1982). Improving the psychometric, criterion-referenced, and practical qualities of integrative language tests. *TESOL Quarterly, 16*(3), 367–379.
Hadley, G., & Mort, J. (1999). An investigation of interrater reliability in oral testing. Nagaoka National College of Technology. Available: http://www.nuis.ac.jp/~hadley/publication/interrater/reliability.htm
Hadley, G., & Naaykens, J. (1999). Testing the test: Comparing SEMAC and exact word scoring on the selective deletion Cloze. *The Korea TESOL Journal, 2*(1), 63–72. Available: http://www2.human.niigata-u.ac.jp/~ghadley/main/resources/Publications/Hadley-Naaykens-KOTESOL.pdf
Kormos, J., & Denes, M. (2004). Exploring measures and perceptions of fluency in the speech of second language learners. *System, 32,* 145–164.
Wang, P. (2009). The inter-rater reliability in scoring composition. *CCSE English Language Teaching, 2*(3), 39–43. Available: http://www.ccsenet.org/journal/index.php/elt/issue/view/174
Wilson, D. V. (2012). Developing a placement exam for Spanish heritage language learners: item analysis and learner characteristics. *Heritage Language Journal, 9*(1), 27–50.

2. Using the journal article you found for application task #1, answer these questions:

What correlation was used? Was any reason given for why that particular correlation was used?

Were the assumptions identified and reported? Which assumptions? Which assumptions were not dealt with?

How was normal distribution determined? What do you think? Given the information provided, do you think the distributions of the variables were normal? Given the variables that the author or authors correlated, would you have expected a positive or a negative correlation? Why? What were the correlation coefficients and *P*-values? Pick the highest (positive or negative) and the lowest correlations and interpret them. Was effect size discussed? If not, calculate the effect size or effect sizes of at least two correlations. Interpret the effect sizes.

3. In Textbook Table 7.4 shows data used for the Spearman's rank-order correlation example. Are the data for each of the variables normally distributed or do they have nonnormal distributions? Or is one of them normally distributed and the other not? Calculate descriptive statistics for each variable, including test range, mean, median, mode, standard deviation, minimum, maximum, kurtosis, and skewness. Use the results to argue whether Pearson's product-moment correlation could have been used, or whether Spearman's rank order correlation should be used. Show your work.

4. The following application task is based on the oral performance test offered by Hadley, G., & Mort, J. (1999). An investigation of interrater reliability in oral testing. Nagaoka National College of Technology. Available: http://www.nuis.ac.jp/~hadley/publication/interrater/reliability.htm

   Note that with this instrument, the test makers multiply each criterion, such as communicative ability, by a certain factor ("x 6") so as to add up to 100%. However, for the purposes of estimating interrater reliability, we will use only the raw ratings (0, 1, 2, 3, 4, 5) added up to a raw total for each test candidate (see Student Workbook Figure 7.1).

   Student Workbook Table 7.2 shows data from two test administrations. Calculate inter-rater reliability for raters 1 and 2 for student group number 1 and for raters 3 and 4 for student group number 2. What is the correlation coefficient? How would you interpret the coefficients? How would you act on this information?

   BONUS: Can you detect any rater bias? Hint: You might ask an American speaker of English to identify the students' names in terms of their gender.

Speaking Test Evaluation Sheet

Total Score: _____

Name _____

Student Number _____

Class _____

Scale

		Description	Scale
a	Communicative Ability:	Includes length of utterances, Flexibility to speakers of differing levels. Complexity of responses. (x 6)	0 • 1 • 2 • 3 • 4 • 5
b	Fluency:	Appropriate Speed, Pauses, and Discourse Stategies. (x 4)	0 • 1 • 2 • 3 • 4 • 5
c	Vocabulary:	Did the student use a wide variety of words and phrases, or use new vocabulary learned in class? (x 3)	0 • 1 • 2 • 3 • 4 • 5
d	Nonverbal Strategies:	Did the student supplement oral communication with appropriate gestures, eye contact and body language? (x 3)	0 • 1 • 2 • 3 • 4 • 5
e	Grammar:	How accurate and appropriate was the student's grammar (x 2)	0 • 1 • 2 • 3 • 4 • 5
f	Pronunciation:	Was effort made to use correct intonation, or was the accent a barrier to communication? (x 2)	0 • 1 • 2 • 3 • 4 • 5

Scoring Guide

0 - 15: Repeatedly communicates in first language or uses first language strategies.	60 - 69%: Learner is making a sincere attempt to communicate. Although discourse causes cognitive strain for a native speaker, he/she can understand most of what is said.
16% - 29%: Unintelligible and incoherent.	70 - 79%: Good communicative ability. Fairly fluent, uses new vocabulary, grammar & pronunciation are adequate.
30% - 49%: Mostly unintelligible. However, a native speaker *might* understand some of what learner is saying, but only after considerable effort.	80 - 89%: Superior communicative ability and fluency. Uses new vocabulary, mostly accurate grammar & pronunciation, good use of non-verbal strategies.
50% - 59%: Somewhat understandable. Discourse seems non-communicative and memorized only for the examination.	90 - 100%: Excellent communicative ability. Language skills are no longer a barrier to communication.

Figure 7.1. Speaking Text Evaluation Sheet.

Table 7.2.
Descriptive Statistics for Application Task 4

Student Group #1 Names	Rater 1 Total Raw Scores	Rater 2 Total Raw Scores	Student Group #2 Names	Rater 3 Raw Scores	Rater 4 Raw Scores
Pete	29	20	Marian	30	29
Carol	29	30	Karen	29	30
Alice	27	28	Georgia	27	27
Bob	26	24	Geoff	27	26
Norma	24	24	Alex	26	27
Joe	24	20	Jacob	26	28
Bud	22	18	Peter	25	25
Louise	19	24	Theresa	25	27
Donna	17	23	John	20	21
Kenny	15	14	Neil	18	19
Julianne	14	20	Sharon	17	18
Marie	8	18	Adam	16	15
			Dick	16	15
			Joan	8	9

5. Student Workbook Table 7.3 shows dataset for a unit vocabulary test that has been dichotomously scored. Calculate point-biserial correlation for each item. You can use either the "classic" formula found in Pett (1997) (see Textbook Figure 7.3), or you can use the "alternate" item-to-whole. What is your interpretation of the results for each item? What actions can you take to improve the test?

Table 7.3.
Student Workbook Unit Vocabulary Test Dataset

Student Name	Item 1	Item 2	Item 3	Item 4	Item 5	Item 6	Item 7	Item 8	Item 9	Item 10	Total Score
Felix	0	1	1	1	1	1	1	1	1	1	9
Waltraud	0	1	1	1	1	1	1	1	1	1	9
Christina	1	1	1	0	1	1	0	1	1	1	8
Gisa	1	0	1	1	1	1	0	1	1	1	8
Halge	0	1	1	1	1	1	1	0	1	1	8
Benno	0	1	0	1	1	1	0	1	1	1	7

(Table continues on next page)

Table 7.3.
Vocabulary Test Dataset (Continued)

Student Name	Item 1	Item 2	Item 3	Item 4	Item 5	Item 6	Item 7	Item 8	Item 9	Item 10	Total Score
Dolf	1	1	0	0	1	1	0	1	1	1	7
Erich	0	1	0	1	1	1	1	1	1	0	7
Gerhard	1	0	0	1	1	1	1	0	1	1	7
Elke	1	1	0	0	1	1	0	1	1	1	7
Gisela	0	1	1	0	1	1	1	0	1	1	7
Hedda	0	1	1	1	0	0	1	1	1	1	7
Bettina	0	0	1	1	1	1	0	1	1	1	7
Alex	1	1	0	0	1	1	0	0	1	1	6
Erwin	0	1	1	0	1	1	0	0	1	1	6
Agathe	0	1	0	0	0	1	1	1	1	1	6
Gabi	0	1	0	1	1	1	1	0	1	0	6
Adel	1	1	0	0	0	1	1	0	1	0	5
Andrea	0	1	0	0	0	1	0	0	1	1	4

BONUS: Can you make an argument for simply using the B-index for this short test, instead of using point-biserial? Where would you place the cut point? Why?

TEST YOURSELF ANSWERS

1. What are at least two ways you can use correlation in testing?
   Correlation can be used to estimate inter-rater reliability and also examine the contribution of individual items to the total score of a test, much like item discrimination or b-index.

2. What is positive correlation? What would a positive correlation coefficient look like?
   An increase in one variable indicates a similar increase in another variable. A positive correlation would look something like .19 or .83, up to a maximum of 1.00.

3. What is negative correlation? What would a negative correlation coefficient look like?
   An increase in one variable indicates a decrease in another variable. A negative correlation would look something like −.16 or −.67, up to a maximum of −1.00.

4. Are negative correlations bad? Why or why not?
   They are not necessarily bad. Some events in a language classroom or in language learning are going to be negatively correlated. One possible example: As learners' confusion or anxiety increases, their achievement may decrease. Or, as learners' homesickness or culture shock increases, the less they talk to their homestay families, in the case of study abroad. Gains in one area of language use, such as speaking fluency, may result in less grammatical accuracy or a more narrow working vocabulary repertoire.

5. What are the names of three correlation procedures?
   Pearson product-moment correlation, point-biserial correlation, and Spearman rank-order correlation.

6. Which correlations are parametric? In what situations would you use them?
   Pearson product-moment correlation and point-biserial correlation are considered parametric measures. They should be used when at least one of the variables, if not both, have normal distributions.

7. Which correlation is nonparametric? In what situation would you use it?
   Spearman rank-order correlation is considered to be a nonparametric measure. It is used when one or both of the variables have clearly nonnormal distributions.

8. What is an assumption? Why are they important?
   This is an operating condition or requirement of a given statistical procedure. If multiple assumptions are not met, then a TREE may get misleading results.

9. What is causality? What is the relevance of the idea of causality to correlation?
   A strong connection between two variables such that we can identify one variable as the source of a second variable. One causes the other. Simply estimating a correlation coefficient does not establish causality. Rather, it is theory and reason that do so.

10. What is effect size?
    This is the strength, or meaningfulness, of the result of a statistical procedure such as correlation. In correlation, the coefficient of determination suggests how much variance is directly shared between two variables.

11. Name the assumptions of Pearson product-moment correlation.
    Independence of the two variables, both variables have an interval scale, one or both variables have a normal distribution, the two variables have a linear relationship, and the two variables have equal variance.

12. Describe the two kinds of variables needed to use point-biserial correlation.
    One of the variables much be dichotomously scored (right or wrong), whereas the other must have an interval scale.

13. In what circumstances would you use Spearman rank-order correlation?
    If one or both of the variables had clearly nonnormal distributions, as evidenced by descriptive statistics along with histograms. When in doubt, it is acceptable to calculate both Spearman rank-order and Pearson product-moment correlations and report both.

14. How do you get the kind of scales needed for Spearman rank-order correlation?
    Interval scale data are mathematically converted to rank scale data by arranging learners from highest to lowest score. Tie scores are added and averaged.

15. What are two measures that tell us the strength of a correlation?
    The correlation coefficient itself (r) and the coefficient of determination (R^2).

16. What is a *P*-value and what is it used for?
    P stands for "probability." When a correlation coefficient is estimated, it is checked for statistical significance—in other words, to estimate the probability of whether the correlation is simply the result of random chance. The conventional *P*-value threshold for statistical significance is $P < .05$.

Second Language Testing for Student Evaluation and Classroom Research 79

DISCUSSION QUESTIONS ANSWERS

1. Correlation is a commonly used statistical procedure in testing and research. What kind of experience have you had using correlation? Or, have you read reports than mention using it? What connections can you make between your previous experience and this chapter?
It is unknown what your response will be. Many evaluation and research studies use correlation, particularly if tests and/or questionnaires comprise the data-collection instruments. To the extent you have read evaluation or research reports, you may have some familiarity. We would guess, however, that Chapter 7 provides more specific knowledge of how to interpret correlation coefficients. We also think that many TREEs have intuitions (these are teacher theories, in many ways) about what affects learning (learner motivation, learner time spent at study, how often vocabulary are recycled, learner attendance). If a TREE can figure out how to capture these constructs in tests, questionnaires, or observations, he or she can test his or her hypotheses using correlation.

2. List five pairs of variables you would like to correlate. Use Student Workbook Table 7.1 and share your answers with a classmate. Write down their feedback.
We think TREEs have intuitions about events and behaviors in the classroom, and learning. We cannot tell you what these should be. We think, however, that getting a colleague's or a classmate's feedback is essential, particularly in order to address the question of "How do we capture 'motivation?'" Or whatever construct you wish to capture? Filling the fourth column under "Classmate's feedback" should be a prerequisite to successful completion of this discussion question.

3. The text lists assumptions for each of the three correlations. What are the assumptions the three correlations have in common? Are any of the assumptions unique to one or two of the correlations? Which of these assumptions do you feel most confident exploring? Which of these assumptions do you feel least confident exploring?
All three correlation types stipulate, or strongly imply, independence, a linear relationship between variables, and the idea that the variables must be paired. For independence, one cannot correlate a variable with itself. Without a linear relationship, as seen on a scatterplot for Textbook Figures 7.4a and 7.4b, there can be no correlation. Change in one variable has to be matched by similar change in the other, which is what a scatterplot reveals. Finally, to be correlated, learners have to have taken both measures. You cannot correlate two measures taken

by two different groups of learners. All three correlation types stipulate particular types of scales for their variables, although all three assume different types of scales (interval and interval, interval and dichotomous, etc.). Both Pearson product-moment correlation and point-biserial correlation assume normal distributions and equality of variance for both variables, but Spearman rank-order correlation does not. Point-biserial correlation assumes equality of variance for the interval scale within both levels (1s and 0s) of the dichotomous variable.

In terms of exploring normal distribution and equality of variance assumptions, TREEs may feel more confident working with Pearson product-moment correlation. Only two sets of descriptive statistics need to be estimated. They may feel less confident working with point-biserial correlation in terms of these same assumptions. For example, for the data in application task #5, there are 10 items. Using the classic point-biserial formula (Textbook Figure 7.3) descriptive statistics need to be calculated for the interval scale scores for each item, but then also for the total test scores for all learners who got an 0 on that item, and for all learners who got a 1 on that item. To illustrate: For item 1, the mean on the whole test for the seven learners getting item 1 right (the "1" group) was 6.83 and the *SD* was 1.17. The mean on the whole test for the 12 learners getting item 1 wrong (the "0" group) was 6.83 and the *SD* was 1.47. The mean for all learners taking the test was 6.90 and the *SD* was 1.24. It takes some work, and it is conceptually tricky. TREEs working only on item analysis might legitimately forgo checking these assumptions minutely and simply calculate point-biserial correlations but then also item discrimination or b-index, depending on test type (NRT vs. CRT). Of course, if point-biserial correlation is being used for research purposes (e.g., comparing males and females) and not for item analysis, then working with point-biserial correlation and its assumptions becomes necessary.

4. In second and foreign language testing, we often have small sample sizes and nonnormal distributions. Does it necessarily follow that we have to use a nonparametric correlation? How should we decide? There is often enough variance in our tests and other variables for us to use parametric correlations. Descriptive statistics always need to be estimated, and we need to make judgments based on them as to whether we need to use parametric and/or nonparametric statistical procedures. There is nothing wrong with reporting both parametric and nonparametric correlations as long as you explain why you did it, which are accepting as "true," and why.

5. This question builds on discussion question #2. Do you think there may be a third variable Z that would affect any of the X and Y variables you would like to correlate?
We can usually think of third and fourth variables that may affect our original two variables, X and Y. The more studies we read that deal with theories of motivation, anxiety, learning, time on task, intensity and duration of instruction, and so on, the more variables we may be able to identify. The real challenge is how to capture the variables in our tests, and so on.

6. As if to a colleague or a supervisor, explain what *P*-values should and should not be used for.
P-values are useful for determining whether a correlation is statistically significant or not, or whether the correlation is simply an accident. We use the *P*-value to decide "yes an accident" or "no, probably not an accident." We then use the correlation coefficient and an effect size to decide whether the relationship between the two variables actually mean anything, and whether we can act on them in some way.

7. What points about correlation remain unclear to you? Write them here and ask about them during class or office hours, or through your own reading.
It is unknown what your response will be. Many TREEs have an intuitive idea of relationships between events and activities in learners' lives, and actual learning, but may be unclear how to capture these constructs. Also, when confronted by formulae such as that for point-biserial correlation, some TREEs may feel unclear how to proceed, or how to put into action what they wish to do.

8. What points about correlation do you feel clear about, that you can explain or use with confidence? Consider offering to teach it to your classmates or review it with them using your own data.
It is unknown what your response will be. We hope you will have some questions to ask, and strategies for finding the answers, and that you can assist your colleagues with basic correlations. Even though your explanation or demonstration of correlation may be rocky or incomplete, the experience will let you know what you are more, or less, clear on.

APPLICATION TASKS ANSWERS

1. Retrieve one of the following articles using correlation. Many online articles become unavailable, due to the dynamic nature of

the internet. You should learn how to use the document retrieval capabilities of academic libraries near you. Many online articles which have become unavailable may still be available through your library document retrieval system. Further, do not avoid an article just because the date makes it seem "old." Inquiry such as that done by Currall and Kirk (1986) and Cziko (1982), for example, is never dated.

Currall, S., & Kirk, R. (1986). Predicting success in intensive foreign language courses. *The Modern Language Journal, 70*(2), 107–113.

Cziko, G. (1982). Improving the psychometric, criterion-referenced, and practical qualities of integrative language tests. *TESOL Quarterly, 16*(3), 367–379.

Hadley, G., & Mort, J. (1999). An investigation of interrater reliability in oral testing. Nagaoka National College of Technology. Available: http://www.nuis.ac.jp/~hadley/publication/interrater/reliability.htm

Hadley, G., & Naaykens, J. (1999). Testing the test: Comparing SEMAC and exact word scoring on the selective deletion Cloze. *The Korea TESOL Journal, 2*(1), 63–72. Available: http://www2.human.niigata-u.ac.jp/~ghadley/main/resources/Publications/Hadley-Naaykens-KOTESOL.pdf

Kormos, J., & Denes, M. (2004). Exploring measures and perceptions of fluency in the speech of second language learners. *System, 32,* 145–164.

Wang, P. (2009). The inter-rater reliability in scoring composition. *CCSE English Language Teaching, 2*(3), 3–43. Available: http://www.ccsenet.org/journal/index.php/elt/issue/view/174

Wilson, D. V. (2012). Developing a placement exam for Spanish heritage language learners: item analysis and learner characteristics. *Heritage Language Journal, 9*(1), 27–50.

Successful completion of this task is to have the full article in hand or in electronic form.

2. Using the journal article you found for application task #1, answer these questions:

What correlation was used? Was any reason given why that particular correlation was used?
If a particular type of correlation was not named or reasons for it, this should be stated.

Were the assumptions identified and reported? Which assumptions? Which assumptions were not dealt with?
Assumptions for correlations are not often reported, unless the author(s) could not use Pearson product-moment. If the assumptions are not discussed, this should be stated for this task.

How was normal distribution determined? What do you think? Given the information provided, do you think the distributions of the variables were normal?
At the very least, the descriptive statistics should be reported for variables. Given the mean, standard deviation, and test range, you can probably guess in a rough way whether the variables are normally distributed, whether the author(s) did or not.

Given the variables that the author or authors correlated, would you have expected a positive or a negative correlation? Why?
A successful response to this question will include a brief explanation of what is being correlated, a hypothesis as to whether a correlation would be positive or negative, and most importantly, your own reasons behind the hypothesis.

What were the correlation coefficients and *P*-values? Pick the highest (positive or negative) and the lowest correlations and interpret them.
Check your interpretations with classmates and your instructor.

Was effect size discussed? If not, calculate the effect size or effect sizes of at least two correlations. Interpret the effect sizes.
Use the coefficient of determination to determine effect sizes. Multiply the correlation coefficient with itself to get R^2. Write out your interpretations and check with them classmates, colleagues, and/or your instructor.

3. In Table 7.4 of the textbook shows data used for the Spearman's rank-order correlation example. Are the data for each of the variables normally distributed, or do they have non-normal distributions? Or is one of them normally distributed, and the other not? Calculate descriptive statistics for each variable, including test range, mean, median, mode, standard deviation, minimum, maximum, kurtosis, and skewness.

Use the results to argue whether Pearson's product-moment correlation could have been used, or whether Spearman's rank order correlation should be used. Show your work. Student Workbook Table 7.4 shows the descriptive statistics for the interval scale data in Table 7.4 of the textbook. Even though this is a small sample size ($N = 12$), we can see the distributions for tests X and Y are somewhat normal. Test X has a slightly flat distribution and a large standard deviation relative to the test range, yet skewness and kurtosis are within the range of normal (Appendix C). Test Y has a negative skew that almost reaches the threshold of nonnormality using the standard error of skewness and Fisher's Error of Skewness (Appendix C). Test Y also has a peaked distribution that almost reaches the threshold of nonnormality. It is probably reasonable to use a nonparametric statistical procedure on this data.

4. The following application task is based on the oral performance test offered by Hadley, G., & Mort, J. (1999). An investigation of interrater reliability in oral testing. Nagaoka National College of Technology. Available: http://www.nuis.ac.jp/~hadley/publication/interrater/reliability.htm

Table 7.4.
Student Workbook Descriptive Statistics for Application Task 4

Descriptive Statistic	Interval Scale Data on Test X	Interval Scale Data on Test Y
N	12	12
Test score range	10	60
Mean	6.17	45
Median	5	45
Mode	5	45
Max	10	50
Min	2	35
Standard deviation	2.52	4.26
Skewness	.10	−1.05
Standard Error of Skewness (Brown)	.71	.71
Standard Error of Skewness (alternate)	.64	.64
Fisher's Skewness coefficient (using alternate SES)	.16	−1.64
Kurtosis	−1.20	1.93
Standard Error of Kurtosis (Brown)	1.41	1.41
Standard Error of Kurtosis (alternate)	1.23	1.23
Fisher's Kurtosis coefficient (using alternate SEK)	−.98	1.57

Note that with this instrument, the test makers multiply each criterion, such as communicative ability, by a certain factor so as to add up to 100%. However, for the purposes of estimating interrater reliability, we will use only the raw ratings (0, 1, 2, 3, 4, 5) added up to a raw total for each test candidate.

Here are the data from two test administrations. Calculate inter-rater reliability for raters 1 and 2 for student group number 1 and also for raters 3 and 4 for student group number 2. What is the correlation coefficient? How would you interpret the coefficients? How would you act on this information?

BONUS: Can you detect any rater bias? Hint: You might ask an American speaker of English to identify the students' names in terms of their gender.
Raters 1 and 2, r = .60. Raters 3 and 4, r = .99.
The inter-rater reliability for raters 1 and 2 seems low. The raters may understand the scoring criteria differently and/or they are unclear about the criteria or scoring procedure. The inter-rater reliability for raters 3 and 4 is high. It means your rater training was successful and/or your raters understand the criteria in the same way, and consistently so. But because the coefficient is so high, you do need to question how that happened. For instance, you need to ask raters whether they conferred on scores before awarding scores. There may be nothing wrong with this, but raters should not just copy each other. Each test candidate should have a subjective, but principled (based on the criteria), rating by each rater. We note that the dataset shows slightly different ratings for raters 3 and 4. They are not exact copies. The two raters do not completely agree. However, the correlation shows that as one rater increases, so does the other. When one rater gives a lower score, so does the other.

For rater 1, quite a few of the female test candidates are getting lower scores, compared to scores awarded for females by rater 2.

As will be seen in Chapter 8 on reliability, calculating the correlation between raters' scores is only the first of two steps that are needed to estimate inter rater reliability. Yet the correlation alone is an effective first indicator of the level of agreement between raters.

5. Table 7.5 shows a dataset for a unit vocabulary test that has been dichotomously scored. Calculate point-biserial correlation for each item. You can use either the "classic" formula found in Pett (1997)

(see Figure 7.3) or you can use the "alternate" item-to-whole. What is your interpretation of the results for each item? What actions can you take to improve the test?

Table 7.5.
Student Workbook Unit Vocabulary Test Dataset

Student Name	Item 1	Item 2	Item 3	Item 4	Item 5	Item 6	Item 7	Item 8	Item 9	Item 10	Total Score
Felix	0	1	1	1	1	1	1	1	1	1	9
Waltraud	0	1	1	1	1	1	1	1	1	1	9
Christina	1	1	1	0	1	1	0	1	1	1	8
Gisa	1	0	1	1	1	1	0	1	1	1	8
Halge	0	1	1	1	1	1	1	0	1	1	8
Benno	0	1	0	1	1	1	0	1	1	1	7
Dolf	1	1	0	0	1	1	0	1	1	1	7
Erich	0	1	0	1	1	1	1	1	1	0	7
Gerhard	1	0	0	1	1	1	1	0	1	1	7
Elke	1	1	0	0	1	1	0	1	1	1	7
Gisela	0	1	1	0	1	1	1	0	1	1	7
Hedda	0	1	1	1	0	0	1	1	1	1	7
Bettina	0	0	1	1	1	1	0	1	1	1	7
Alex	1	1	0	0	1	1	0	0	1	1	6
Erwin	0	1	1	0	1	1	0	0	1	1	6
Agathe	0	1	0	0	0	1	1	1	1	1	6
Gabi	0	1	0	1	1	1	1	0	1	0	6
Adel	1	1	0	0	0	1	1	0	1	0	5
Andrea	0	1	0	0	0	1	0	0	1	1	4

BONUS: Can you make an argument for simply using the B-index for this short test instead of using point-biserial? Where would you place the cut point? Why?

As promised, an example calculation of the point-biserial correlation formula in Textbook Figure 7.3 is given in Student Workbook Figure 7.2 for item 1 of the dataset.

Step 1, Item 1

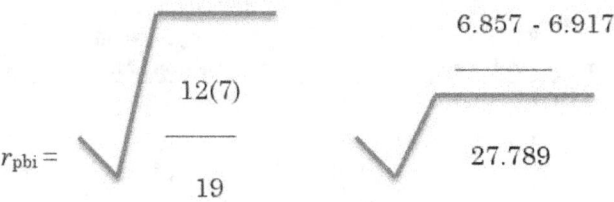

$$r_{\text{pbi}} = \sqrt{\dfrac{12(7)}{19}} \sqrt{\dfrac{6.857 - 6.917}{27.789}}$$

n_0 is the number of learners who are coded 0 on item 1 (12)
n_1 is the number of learners who are coded 1 on item 1 (7)
N is the sample size (19)
M_1 is the total test score mean of learners who are coded 1 on item 1 (8+8+7+7+7+6+5 / 7 = 6.857)
M_0 is the total test score mean of learners who are coded 0 on item 1 (9+9+8+7+7+7+7+7+6+6+6+4 / 12 = 6.917)
Σ is "sum of"
X is each learner's total test score
M is the test score mean of all learners in the sample for all items (6.895)

Figure 7.2. Step 1 for point-biserial correlation application example for Item 1 in Student Workbook Table 7.5.

For the last three elements (Σ, X, M):

Table 7.6.
Learners Total Scores for Point-Biserial Formula Application

Student Name	Student Total Score	Mean Score	Student Score Minus Group Mean	Squared
Felix	9	6.895	2.105	4.432
Waltraud	9	6.895	2.105	4.432
Christiane	8	6.895	1.105	1.221
Gisa	8	6.895	1.105	1.221
Halge	8	6.895	1.105	1.221
Benno	7	6.895	0.105	0.011
Dolf	7	6.895	0.105	0.011
Erich	7	6.895	0.105	0.011
Gerhard	7	6.895	0.105	0.011
Elke	7	6.895	0.105	0.011

(Table continues on next page)

Table 7.6.
Learners Total Scores (Continued)

Student Name	Student Total Score	Mean Score	Student Score Minus Group Mean	Squared
Gisela	7	6.895	0.105	0.011
Hedda	7	6.895	0.105	0.011
Bettina	7	6.895	0.105	0.011
Alex	6	6.895	−0.894	0.800
Erwin	6	6.895	−0.894	0.800
Agathe	6	6.895	−0.894	0.800
Gabi	6	6.895	−0.894	0.800
Adel	5	6.895	−1.894	3.590
Andrea	4	6.895	−2.894	8.379

$\Sigma = 27.789$

Step 2, Item 1

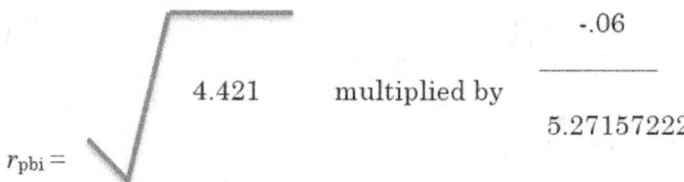

$$r_{pbi} = \sqrt{4.421} \text{ multiplied by } \frac{-.06}{5.27157222}$$

Figure 7.3. Step 2 for point-biserial correlation example in Student Workbook Table 7.8.

Step 3 2.103 multiplied by −.011 = −.024 = r_{pbi}

Here are the answers for the "classic point-biserial correlation formula and the "alternate" item-to-whole correlation method:

Table 7.6.
Student Workbook Comparison of Point-Biserial and Item-to Whole Correlations for All Items

	Item 1	Item 2	Item 3	Item 4	Item 5	Item 6	Item 7	Item 8	Item 9	Item 10
Point-biserial	−.024	−.157	.606	.528	.596	−.021	.179	.543	0	.320
Item-to-whole	−.389	−.421	.235	.134	.306	−.201	−.231	.158	0	.019

It appears that items 1, 2, 6, and 9 are not functioning well. They have low or negative correlations with the rest of the test. Items 3, 4, 5, and 8 appear to be functioning well with moderate positive correlations. They are measuring something similar to the total test. The two different correlation formulae are offering functionally contradictory results for items 7 and 10. By "functionally" different we mean that the point-biserial correlations are suggesting different actions than item-to-whole correlations. Item 7 is likely not functioning, but the point-biserial correlation is .179. It's low but approaching a minimum of .25 to be a good item. Item 10 is the opposite. Point-biserial is saying "good item," but the item-to-whole correlation is saying the item is not functioning. Item 10 does not have a lot of variance (most learners got the item right). Further, the standard deviations of groups 0 and group 1 are different (1 vs. 2.09), meaning they do not have equality of variance. As variables, these may violate the assumptions of point-biserial correlation and Pearson-product moment correlation (recall the item-to-whole correlation is a variation of Pearson). Item 7 is less clear. The two groups (0 and 1) have similar standard deviations (1.225 vs. 1.287). Yet if you move your finger down the column and 1s and 0s on the spreadsheet, it is easy to see that 1s (correct responses) seem equally distributed among high-, middle-, and low-scoring students. An r_{pbi} of .179 suggests a nonfunctioning item, as does item-to-whole r of −.231.

This opens an argument for simply using B-index or item discrimination for test analysis and revision, particularly for smaller datasets. Many also find B-index or item discrimination easier to calculate than point-biserial correlation.

STUDENT WORKBOOK
CHAPTER 8

RELIABILITY

TEST YOURSELF

Working alone or with a study partner, ask and answer these questions:

1. What is reliability?
2. What is the relationship between constructs and reliability?
3. What is an obtained score?
4. What is a true score?
5. What is meaningful variance?
6. What is measurement error? What are some causes of measurement error?
7. What information does a reliability coefficient contain?
8. How is reliability related to test fairness?

Second Language Testing for Student Evaluation and Classroom Research
Student Workbook, pp. 91–114
Copyright © 2018 by Information Age Publishing
All rights of reproduction in any form reserved.

9. How many types of reliability are there?

10. How does someone do repeated measures reliability? What does it measure?

11. How does someone do parallel forms reliability? What does it measure?

12. What are two ways to do internal consistency reliability? What does it measure?

13. What is it Cronbach's alpha can do that other internal consistency reliability estimates cannot do?

14. What is a key feature of rater reliability?

15. What is the difference between inter- and intra-rater reliability?

16. What does SEM stand for?

17. When an SEM is small relative to the test score range, it means reliability is _____ .

18. What is test dependability?

19. What is phi lambda? What is it used for?

20. Name at least three ways to increase test score reliability.

DISCUSSION QUESTIONS ANSWERS

1. As if to a nontesting person, explain what reliability is, and why we should try to get reliable test scores.

2. What are some sources of measurement error? What is one source that might be easy to deal with? What is one source of measurement error that might be hard to deal with, or take more time to deal with?

3. How would you interpret a reliability coefficient of .76 for a paper and ink test?

4. A colleague has a test with 40 items with "right" or "wrong" items. What are two ways your colleague could estimate the test reliability?

5. What if the colleague had a test with 30 "right/wrong" items but then 10 more items that were subjectively scored? What "reliability plan" could you offer to estimate reliability for a test where there are mixed test item formats (objectively scored versus subjectively scored)?

6. Under what conditions might you use KR-21? What are the advantages and disadvantages?

7. Suppose you were working with two raters, and their correlated scores for learners was .61. Even with a Spearman Brown Prophecy correction their estimated reliability was .65. Interpret this coefficient. What could be causing the situation? What could you do about it?

8. Some believe that intra-rater reliability is not as "good" or trustworthy as inter-rater reliability. What steps could you take to ensure that an intra-rater reliability estimation was trustworthy?

9. How is test score reliability related to the standard error of measurement (SEM)? For a test with 25 items and an SEM of 6.00, would you say the SEM is small or large? By extension, if the test likely reliable or unreliable?

10. What are ways you could reduce the amount of reading learners have to do to take a test that is not actually focused on reading?

APPLICATION TASKS

1. Lindsey teaches English as a second language to junior high school students in a rural school. Most of their parents work in the dairy and food processing business nearby. Attendance is generally very good. Her students work hard and seldom miss class. Often they serve as translators for their parents.

   Lindsey recently administered a 20-item test to her students to measure their progress in the course. She was surprised to discover that her test score reliability was only .45 (she used Cronbach's alpha). What might account for the low reliability? Think of at least four reasons.

2. Given your reasons, what specific suggestions can you give to Lindsey to improve her test score reliability?

3. Kai teaches Japanese as a foreign language in a small college in the Midwestern United States. She wants to conduct a research project and wants to make a questionnaire to understand students' attitudes toward learning Japanese. She has heard of something called parallel forms reliability, and has asked you for your opinion. Could you suggest another type of reliability that would better suit her investigation? What reasons could you give for your suggestion?

4. An English as a second-language program director received this e-mail about a student who took a high-stakes performance test and failed. This test was a teaching simulation test.

   Maureen,

   I am concerned about Mr. XXXX. I think he chose too difficult a concept to explain for his teaching simulation, but I feel it needs to be reviewed by you or your supervisor. I think if he gets in the ESL class for teacher preparation, the teacher will wonder why he is even in it. Would it be possible for you to review the video recording and see what you think? If you look past the difficulty of the concept he chose to teach, I hope you will see what I mean. We had one like this last year who after a couple of weeks of class in the teacher preparation class was passed. Fortunately, our teaching assistant coordinator has put him down as "passed" so he got the higher salary.

   Sincerely, Doris

   If you were Maureen, how might you answer this e-mail? As a program director, how would you ensure your performance tests were reliable?

5. Here is Maureen's response.

   Hello Doris,

   Thanks for your e-mail. I got the chance to review the footage from Mr. XXXX's presentation yesterday. I also looked over the score sheets again. After reviewing the materials, I'm confident that the assessment given was a fair and accurate assessment.

I went ahead and took a look at his practice presentation as well, when he gave a presentation on a different topic. It seems that he did improve from his practice performance to his final performance, but not quite enough to pass the assessment. He was close, but didn't quite get there.

The issues that the raters identified where linguistic and didn't stem from the complexity of his topic. His teaching skills are quite good and I'm sure that with some more work with his spoken English he will make an excellent TA. Please let me know if you have anymore questions!

Best,

Maureen

How would you evaluate Maureen's response? Can you think of additional information you might give regarding the reliability of the test?

6. Student Workbook Table 8.1 are some descriptive statistics for three objectively scored tests including k, M, SD, N, min, max, mode, and median. Calculate KR-21 for each test.

Table 8.1.
Descriptive Statistics for Three Tests

	Test 1	Test 2	Test 3*
k	30	50	10
M	23.12	29.118	6.895
SD	4.312	8.131	1.243
N	59	17	19
Min, Max	15, 30	11, 41	4, 9
Mode	23	31	7
Median	23	31	7
Test description	End of unit introduction to language test, U.S. sophomore college students	End of semester EFL vocabulary and listening post-test, second-year Japanese college students	German vocabulary quiz, first-year U.S. college students
KR-21			

*Note. You may get an unusual reliability coefficient for this test.

7. Interpret each coefficient, as if to a nontesting person. Then, answer these questions: How would you account for the different KR-21 reliability coefficients between tests 1 and 2? Would split half or alpha reliability give different results? Why might that be the case? For test 3, assuming there was no mistake in calculating the coefficient, what might cause a negative or zero reliability coefficient?

8. Using the standard deviation and KR-21 reliability coefficients from task 1, calculate the SEM for tests 1 and 2 only from Student Workbook Table 8.1.

Table 8.2.
SEM for Tests 1 and 2

	Test 1	Test 2
Standard error of measure		

9. Interpret the two SEMs. For test 1, the cut score for pass/fail is 22 (learners with 22 points or above pass). For test 2, the cut score is 34. Learners with 34 and above are going to an advanced class. Learners with lower scores repeat the current class.

10. Look at the total scores for test 2 (application task #6 Student Workbook Task 8.1). Enter the scores into a spreadsheet program and in the column to the right (B1) and calculate the proportion scores (=A1/50). Calculate the mean of the proportion scores (M_p), and the standard deviation (using the sample formula) of the proportion scores (SD_p).

Total scores from test 2:

    41
    39
    39
    37
    35
    35
    31
    31
    31

27
26
24
24
22
22
20
11

Then calculate phi lambda dependability at the following proportion cut scores:

$\lambda = .90$ _____

$\lambda = .80$ _____

$\lambda = .70$ _____

$\lambda = .65$ _____

11. Student Workbook Table 8.3 is a final application task for calculating Cronbach's alpha using scores ranging from 1 to 5 on an eight-item questionnaire capturing learners' evaluation of an instructor. Here are two sample questionnaire items:

Please read each item about your instructor and circle your answer:

Table 8.3.
Sample Questionaire Items

1. Gives us a lot of practice in class.				
1	2	3	4	5
Poor	Unsatisfactory	Satisfactory	Very good	Excellent
2. Can explain things in more than one way.				
1	2	3	4	5
Poor	Unsatisfactory	Satisfactory	Very good	Excellent

Student Workbook Table 8.4 is the dataset for the questionaire. On a spreadsheet, each row is one respondent to the questionnaire ($N = 25$). Each column is a questionnaire item.

Table 8.4.
Questionaire Data

Item 1	Item 2	Item 3	Item 4	Item 5	Item 6	Item 7	Item 8
3	3	4	3	3	3	4	3
4	5	4	5	4	5	4	4
5	4	4	4	4	4	4	5
4	4	4	5	4	4	4	4
5	4	4	5	5	5	5	5
5	5	5	5	5	5	5	5
5	5	5	5	5	5	5	4
5	4	5	5	5	5	5	5
3	3	3	4	4	3	3	3
5	5	5	5	5	5	5	5
5	5	5	5	5	5	5	5
3	4	2	3	4	2	1	1
5	5	5	5	5	5	5	5
5	5	5	5	5	5	5	5
5	5	5	3	4	5	5	4
3	2	3	3	3	4	3	3
4	5	5	4	5	4	5	4
5	5	5	5	5	5	5	5
4	4	4	5	5	4	3	4
5	4	5	5	5	4	4	4
5	5	5	5	5	5	5	5
4	4	4	4	4	4	4	4
4	4	4	4	4	4	4	4
5	5	5	5	4	5	5	5
4	4	4	5	5	5	4	4

Using the following spreadsheet template instructions (Student Workbook Table 8.5), calculate Cronbach's alpha for this dataset. How would you interpret the resulting reliability coefficient?

Table 8.5.
Spreadsheet Template for Cronbach's Alpha

Steps	Function	Formula	Result
1.	Create a total score column for odd numbered items (note formula given is for the first row of odd numbered items only, so the formula will need to be extended down to all 25 rows)	=A2+C2+E2+G2	
2.	Create a total score column for even numbered items (note formula given is for the first row of even numbered items only, so the formula will need to be extended down to all 25 rows)	=B2+D2+F2+H2	
3.	Create total score column for all eight items (note formula given is for the first row items only, so the formula will need to be extended down to all 25 rows)	=A2+B2+C2+D2+ E2+F2+G2+H2	
4.	Calculate *SDs* for the three columns (odd, even, total)	=STDEV.S(1st cell in odd total column:last cell in odd total column)	
		=STDEV.S(1st cell in even total column:last cell in even total column)	
		=STDEV.S(1st cell in total column:last cell in total column)	

(Table continues on next page)

Table 8.5.
Spreadsheet Template (Continued)

Steps	Function	Formula	Result
5.	Enter odd *SD* into any cell to the far right at the top, say M1		Type in odd total score SD
6.	Square odd *SD* (use cell M2)	=M1*M1	
7.	Enter even *SD* into cell M3		Type in even total score *SD*
8.	Square even *SD* (use cell M4)	=M4*M4	
9.	Add M2 and M4 (use cell M5)	=M2+M4	
10.	Enter total *SD* (use cell M6)		Type in total score *SD*
11.	Square total *SD* (use call M7)	=M7*M7	
12.	Divide M5 by M7 (use M8)	=M5/M7	
13.	Subtract M8 from 1 (use M9)	=1–M8	
14.	Multiply 2 and M9	=2*M9	

TEST YOURSELF ANSWERS

1. What is reliability?
   In classical measurement terms, reliability or consistency is the measurement of systematic variance (desirable) and random variance (undesirable) in a test administration. In practical terms, it means consistently producing similar results.

2. What is the relationship between constructs and reliability?
   Tests with well-defined constructs (skills, abilities, knowledge, attitudes) and with items written to capture them tend to be more reliable than tests without well-defined constructs. Reliability coefficients tend to be higher when only one construct is being measured (a unidimensional trait).

3. What is an obtained score?
   The scores the learners got when they took a test. Sometimes called observed scores.

4. What is a true score?
   The assumption is that a true score is the average score than one would receive on a test if the test were taken an infinite number of times. The obtained score is the true score plus the measurement error.

5. What is meaningful variance?
   How learners differ from each other in terms of the constructs we hope to measure. Constructs, represented by well-written items, appear as meaningful variance in a reliability coefficient.

6. What is measurement error? What are some causes of measurement error?
   Unexpected, unplanned ways in which learners differ from each other on a test, apart from the constructs we hope to capture. Learners may get conflicting directions, or may not understand the wording of a test item of a test task. They may be tired or upset, or some learners may have studied a major part of the test just before class just by chance, where some learners did not. The test itself may be a source of measurement error, with poorly design items and subtests, or at a difficulty level far higher or lower than the test group's ability level.

7. What information does a reliability coefficient contain?
   It is an estimation of the true score or meaningful variance and error variance. A reliability coefficient of .92 states that 92% of the obtained score variance is the true score and 8% of the variance is error. Typically, reliability coefficients vary from 0 to 1.00.

8. How is reliability related to test fairness?
   Learners deserve to have an accurate estimate of what they know and can do. If we are going to give them grades, place them into levels, or decide whether they get into a program, we should use accurate, consistent, and reliable tests to do so.

9. How many types of reliability are there?
   Aside from Rasch models and item response theory, which we do not deal with, there is: repeated measures reliability, parallel forms reliability, internal consistency reliability, and rater reliability.

10. How does someone do repeated measures reliability? What does it measure?
    Learners take the same test twice within a week or two. The two sets of scores are then correlated. This reliability type looks at the stability of learners' scores over two test occasions.

11. How does someone do parallel forms reliability? What does it measure?
    TREEs design two tests based on the same constructs with the same number of items, subtests, and test item formats. Learners take the two tests and the two score sets are correlated. This reliability type shows to what extent the learners treated the two tests as the same, or different.

12. What are two ways to estimate internal consistency reliability? What does it measure?
    There are more than two ways to estimate internal consistency but we only ask for two. They are: split half reliability with a Spearman Brown Prophecy Correction, inter-correlating items in short subtests with a Spearman Brown Prophecy correction, KR-21, and Cronbach's alpha. Internal consistency measures the extent to which learners' responses within the test correlate to each other, or are related to each other.

13. What is it Cronbach's alpha can do that other internal consistency reliability estimates cannot do?
    Cronbach's alpha can handle items with scaled answers (1, 2, 3, 4, 5) such as level of agreement to a statement, or learner judgments about appropriateness about language, or their certainty about the grammaticality of language. Other internal consistency estimates can handle only dichotomously scored data.

14. What is a key feature of rater reliability?
    The key feature is that learners' performances are each scored twice, either by two different raters, or by the same rater at two different times.

15. What is the difference between inter- and intra-rater reliability?
    Inter-rater reliability is done by two different raters. Intra-rater reliability is done by the same rater, but at two different times with at least a week in between ratings.

16. What does SEM stand for?
    Standard error of measurement.

17. When an SEM is small relative to the test score range, it means reliability is perhaps on the higher side.

18. What is test dependability?
This is another word for reliability with reference to criterion-referenced tests which are assumed to have non-normal distributions. Dependability refers to not only score consistency but also consistency of pass/fail decisions.

19. What is phi lambda? What is it used for?
This is an estimate of the dependability or consistency of a test at specific cut score points.

20. Name at least three ways to increase test score reliability.
Pilot the test and revise it, design and then correlate item pairs, increase the number of items, increase the homogeneity of items, improve performance test rater training, use clearly written performance test criteria, increase the number of learners taking the test, and identify non-functioning items using item analysis or reliability analysis functions on statistical programs.

DISCUSSION QUESTIONS ANSWERS

1. As if to a nontesting person, explain what reliability is, and why we should try to get reliable test scores.
There are several ways you can approach this, but it may help to focus on the ideas of consistency and fairness. Reliable tests are more consistent in measuring what we want to know, and to be fair to learners and others who may read our research, we need to use tests that measure things consistently.

2. How would you interpret a reliability coefficient of .76 for a paper-and-pencil test?
This test appears to have 76% meaningful variance and 24% error variance. Learners are scoring differently than each other on the test partly because of what you are trying measure, but it appears that some of their answers are occurring by chance, where they had a lucky guess, or did not understand some of the test questions or tasks.

3. A colleague has a dichotomously scored test with 40 items. What are two ways your colleague could estimate the test reliability?
If your colleague wants to administer the test twice, she could use repeated measures reliability. She can also use split half, KR-21, or Cronbach's alpha reliability.

4. What if the colleague had a test with 35 dichotomously scored items, but then 5 more items that were subjectively scored? What "reliability plan" could you offer to estimate reliability for a test where there are mixed test item formats (objectively scored vs. subjectively scored)?

   The dichotomously scored items can be checked using internal consistency reliability estimates mentioned in Discussion Question #3. The subjectively scored items can be score by the colleague and then scored again a week later without reference to the first set of scores, or the teacher can score the items, and also ask another colleague to score them, and them compare the scores. See Chapter 2 on test item formats for specific suggestions on scoring subjectively scored items.

5. Under what conditions might you use KR-21? What are the advantages and disadvantages?

   Because KR-21 only requires the mean, the standard deviation, and number of items, KR-21 can be calculated quickly and without item level data (items with 1s and 0s) on a spreadsheet. KR-21 has the disadvantage that it may underestimate reliability when items in a test differ from each other in difficulty.

6. Suppose you were working with two raters, and their correlated scores for learners was .61. Even with a Spearman Brown Prophecy correction their estimated reliability was .65. Interpret this coefficient. What could be causing the situation? What could you do about it?

   The raters do not agree with other when reading the same writing samples, or viewing the same oral performances. While one rater scores high, another rater scores low, or when one rater stays the same, the other rater scores high or low. The raters likely have different conceptions of the performance test criteria. They may be unclear on the criteria, or they may have beliefs that are inconsistent with the criteria. Rater training is thought to be the best way to increase rater reliability.

7. Some believe that intra-rater reliability is not as "good" or trustworthy as inter-rater reliability. What steps could you take to ensure that an intra-rater reliability estimation was trustworthy?

   To increase trust in an intra-rater reliability situation, a TREE can ensure that he or she does not know the names of the learners while they are rating, a TREE can wait a week to ten days before doing the second rating, and a TREE can change the order of the performances he or she rates.

8. For a test with 25 items and an SEM of 6.00, would you say the SEM is small or large? By extension, is the test likely reliable or unreliable?

   A standard error of measurement of 6.00 seems large for a 25-item test. A learner getting a score of 18 would have a 68% chance of get a score anywhere from 12 to 24 if she took the test again multiple times. The test is likely unreliable, in that there is so much measurement error relative to the length of the test.

9. What are ways you could reduce the amount of reading learners have to do to take a test that is not actually focused on reading?

   You may have some of your own ideas. We have some suggestions. Reduce the length of the item prompts and distractors, and use more pictures or diagrams instead of words. Make the directions short and clear, or demonstrate the directions when giving the test. Use shorter sentences, and more common vocabulary.

APPLICATION TASKS ANSWERS

1. Lindsey teaches English as a second language to junior high school students in a rural school. Most of their parents work in the dairy and food processing business nearby. Attendance is generally very good. Her students work hard and seldom miss class. Often they serve as translators for their parents.

   Lindsey recently administered a 20-item test to her students to measure their progress in the course. She was surprised to discover that her test score reliability was only .45 (she used Cronbach's alpha). What might account for the low reliability? Think of at least four reasons. What are the implications for the test scores from such a test?

   You may have additional ideas, but here are some suggestions:

   Environment: Check weather conditions about the time of the test. Also check to see whether there was any labor unrest or unusual conditions that might have required the presence of some of her students to act as translators.

   Examinees: Were the students sick, tired, hungry, or emotionally drained just before or during the test? Check to see whether students or families had health conditions. Was the flu going around? Ask other teachers whether they are aware of anything affecting students and/or parent's lives around the time test was given.

Test items: If Lindsey's test uses objective scoring, she could calculate IF and DI and the B-Index (one administration) looking for low-performing items. Is there any pattern? Can she tell what is it about those low-performing items that confuse students? Then, based on results, she could revise test and, if possible, give it later in the semester or as a mid-term or final to check results.

Test procedure: Did the learners understand the test directions? Did they know how to answer the questions, just in terms of the mechanics of taking the test? Was the test given on a computer?

Implication for the test results: The low alpha reliability means Lindsey could not defend her grades and, therefore, probably should not use the test for grading purposes but consider it a pilot.

2. Kai teaches Japanese as a foreign language in a small college in the Midwestern United States. She wants to conduct a research project and wants to make a questionnaire to understand students' attitudes toward learning Japanese. She has heard of something called parallel forms reliability and has asked you for your opinion. Could you suggest another type of reliability that would better suit her investigation? What reasons could you give for your suggestion?

    You may have your own ideas, but here are some suggestions to consider. Each type of reliability coefficient measures a different aspect of error. Parallel forms reliability is only useful if she wants to make two questionnaires that she believes measure the same thing. But then you would have to ask, why have two different forms of the same questionnaire? If Kai is interested in measuring a construct, for example, attitudes toward studying Japanese, then internal consistency is more appropriate.

3. An English as a second-language program director received this e-mail about a student who took a high-stakes performance test and failed. This test was a teaching simulation test.

    ```
    Maureen,

    I am concerned about Mr. XXXX. I think he chose too
    difficult a concept to explain for his teaching simu-
    lation, but I feel it needs to be reviewed by you
    or your supervisor. I think if he gets in the ESL
    class for teacher preparation, the teacher will won-
    der why he is even in it. Would it be possible for
    you to review the video recording and see what you
    think? If you look past the difficulty of the concept
    he chose to teach, I hope you will see what I mean.
    We had one like this last year who after a couple of
    ```

weeks of class in the teacher preparation class was passed. Fortunately, our teaching assistant coordinator has put him down as "passed" so he got the higher salary.

Sincerely, Doris

4. If you were Maureen, how might you answer this e-mail? As a program director, how would you ensure your performance tests were reliable?
You may have your own ideas on answering this ticklish e-mail. But we have some suggestions. Maureen could answer by recounting the ways in which reliability is established for the performance test. She could begin by describing how two independent raters score the same performances, how much rater training is done, and how she has checked the video-recording herself (doing an abbreviated form of intra-rater reliability). She can also argue that the performance test criteria are clearly written and based in theory.

5. Here is Maureen's response.

Hello Doris,

Thanks for your email. I got the chance to review the footage from Mr. XXXX's presentation yesterday. I also looked over the score sheets again. After reviewing the materials, I'm confident that the assessment given was a fair and accurate assessment.

I went ahead and took a look at his practice presentation as well, when he gave a presentation on a different topic. It seems that he did improve from his practice performance to his final performance, but not quite enough to pass the assessment. He was close, but didn't quite get there.

The issues that the raters identified where linguistic and didn't stem from the complexity of his topic. His teaching skills are quite good and I'm sure that with some more work with his spoken English he will make an excellent TA. Please let me know if you have anymore questions!
Best,

Maureen

How would you evaluate Maureen's response? Can you think of additional information you might give regarding the reliability of the test?

Again, you may have your own ideas, but we think this response was strong in some ways. Maureen does not mention the term "reliability" although she talks of accuracy of the test. She demonstrates consistency in interpreting the data by looking at two video-recordings of the learner explaining two different concepts, done two weeks apart. She notes the consistency of the raters' concerns from one test performance to the next, and she also mentions checking through the scoring sheets herself. So the strength of her answer lies in the consistency of her testing procedures, rather than the technical senses of reliability. She might have described the inter-rater reliability for the raters, and the rater training done for the test, but in fact her response is appropriate in that it is not overly technical.

6. In Student Workbook Table 8.1 are some descriptive statistics for three objectively scored tests including k, M, SD, N, min, max, mode, and median. Calculate KR-21 for each test.

Table 8.6.
Descriptive Statistics for Three Tests

	Test 1	Test 2	Test 3*
k	30	50	10
M	23.12	29.118	6.895
SD	4.912	8.131	1.243
N	59	17	19
Min, Max	15, 30	11, 41	4, 9
Mode	23	31	7
Median	23	31	7
Test description	End of unit introduction to language test, U.S. sophomore college students	End of semester EFL vocabulary and listening post-test, second-year Japanese college students	German vocabulary quiz, first-year U.S. college students
KR-21	.739	.832	−.429

*Note. You may get an unusual reliability coefficient for this test.

7. Interpret each coefficient, as if to a nontesting person. Then answer these questions: How would you account for the different KR-21 reliability coefficients between tests 1 and 2? Would split half or alpha reliability give different results? Why might that be the case? For test 3, assuming there was no mistake in calculating the coefficient, what might cause a negative or zero reliability coefficient?

   Test 1 appears to be reasonably reliable, although 26.1% of the variance (the difference between students' scores) is due to error measurement. Perhaps all of the items are not consistently measuring what the test writer intends. Test 1 also has only 30 items. More items might result in a higher reliability coefficient, although the items should be examined using item analysis. Some items might be revised or thrown out, resulting in higher reliability. Test 1 has a somewhat large standard deviation for a 30-item test which suggests that the learners found some items easy and other items difficult. This may result in a low KR-21 reliability, which assumes items have equal difficulty. Test 2 is more reliable than test 1, although 16.8% of the variance is due to error measurement. Test 2 might have better items, which means the test writer may have a clearer idea of what he or she wishes to measure. Test 2 also has more items, which may explain some of the higher reliability. KR-21 is thought to be a conservative measure of reliability and will underestimate internal consistency. Split half and alpha reliability might result in higher reliability coefficients.

   Test 3 may have a negative reliability coefficient because the items may have no relationship to each other. In other words, the learners do not treat the items the same way, as though they are not measuring the same things. Some of the test items may be negatively correlated to each other, or negatively correlated with the total score on the quiz. In Chapter 7 on the Student Workbook, Application Task 5, we see the same data, and items 1, 2, 6, and 9 are not at all related to the rest of the quiz items. Since internal consistency reliability depends on correlation, and if item correlations are negative or zero, any reliability estimate will be very low. Any negative reliability coefficient, if it is not due to calculation errors, should be reported as "zero reliability."

8. Using the standard deviation and KR-21 reliability coefficients from task 1 above, calculate the **SEM** for tests 1 and 2 only from Student Workbook Table 8.1/Table 8.6.

Table 8.7.
SEM for Tests 1 and 2

	Test 1	Test 2
Standard error of measure	2.203	3.334

9. Interpret the two SEMs.
   For test 1, the cut score for pass/fail is 22 (learners with 22 points or above pass). For test 2, the cut score is 34. Learners with 34 and above are going to an advanced class. Learners with lower scores repeat the current class.
   For test 1, a "failing" learner getting a score of 21 has a 68% chance of getting a score as low as 18.8 (or 19 if you round up) OR as high as 23.2 (or 23 if you round down). For test 2, an "advanced" learner getting a score of 36 has a 68% chance of getting a score as low as 32.67 (or 33 if you round up) OR as high as 39.33 (or 39 if you round down). In both tests, additional information from the learners might be needed before deciding to fail learners, or put them into different levels.

10. Look at the total scores for test 2 (application task #6 Student Workbook Tables 8.1/8.2). Enter the scores into a spreadsheet program and in the column to the right (B1) and calculate the proportion scores (=A1/50). Calculate the mean of the proportion scores (M_p), and the standard deviation (using the sample formula) of the proportion scores (SD_p).

Table 8.8.
Total Scores and Proportion Scores for Student Workbook Dataset Table 8.1

Total Scores From Test 2	Proportion Scores
41	0.82
39	0.78
39	0.78
37	0.74
35	0.7
35	0.7
31	0.62
31	0.62
31	0.62

(Table continues on next page)

Table 8.8.
Total Scores and Proportion Scores (Continued

Total Scores From Test 2	Proportion Scores
27	0.54
26	0.52
24	0.48
24	0.48
22	0.44
22	0.44
20	0.4
11	0.22
	Mp = .58235294
	SDp = .16261647

Then calculate phi lambda dependability at the following proportion cut scores:

$\lambda = .90$ .965

$\lambda = .80$ .94

$\lambda = .70$ .89

$\lambda = .65$ .857

11. Student Workbook Table 8.9 is a final application task for calculating Cronbach's alpha using scores ranging from 1 to 5 on an eight-item questionnaire capturing learners' evaluation of an instructor. Here are two sample questionnaire items:

Table 8.3.
Sample Questionaire Items

1. Gives us a lot of practice in class.				
1	2	3	4	5
Poor	Unsatisfactory	Satisfactory	Very good	Excellent

2. Can explain things in more than one way.				
1	2	3	4	5
Poor	Unsatisfactory	Satisfactory	Very good	Excellent

Table 8.4.
Questionaire Data

Item 1	Item 2	Item 3	Item 4	Item 5	Item 6	Item 7	Item 8
3	3	4	3	3	3	4	3
4	5	4	5	4	5	4	4
5	4	4	4	4	4	4	5
4	4	4	5	4	4	4	4
5	4	4	5	5	5	5	5
5	5	5	5	5	5	5	5
5	5	5	5	5	5	5	4
5	4	5	5	5	5	5	5
3	3	3	4	4	3	3	3
5	5	5	5	5	5	5	5
5	5	5	5	5	5	5	5
3	4	2	3	4	2	1	1
5	5	5	5	5	5	5	5
5	5	5	5	5	5	5	5
5	5	5	3	4	5	5	4
3	2	3	3	3	4	3	3
4	5	5	4	5	4	5	4
5	5	5	5	5	5	5	5
4	4	4	5	5	4	3	4
5	4	5	5	5	4	4	4
5	5	5	5	5	5	5	5
4	4	4	4	4	4	4	4
4	4	4	4	4	4	4	4
5	5	5	5	4	5	5	5
4	4	4	5	5	5	4	4

Using the following spreadsheet template instuctions (Student Workbook Table 8.9), calulate Cronbach's Alpha for this data set. How would you interpret the resulting reliability coefficient?

Table 8.9.
Spreadsheet Template for Cronbach's Alpha

Steps	Function	Formula	Result
1.	Create a total score column for odd numbered items (note formula given is for the first row of odd numbered items only, so the formula will need to be extended down to all 25 rows)	=A2+C2+E2+G2	There is only space here to show the first five rows: 14 16 17 16 19 . . .
2.	Create a total score column for even numbered items (note formula given is for the first row of even numbered items only, so the formula will need to be extended down to all 25 rows)	=B2+D2+F2+H2	There is only space here to show the first five rows: 12 19 17 17 19 . . .
3.	Create total score column for all eight items (note formula given is for the first row items only, so the formula will need to be extended down to all 25 rows)	=A2+B2+C2+D2+E2+F2+G2+H2	There is only space here to show the first five rows: 26 35 34 33 38 . . .

(Table continues on next page)

Table 8.9.
Spreadsheet Template (Continued)

Steps	Function	Formula	Result
4.	Calculate *SDs* for the three columns (odd, even, total)	=STDEV.S(1st cell in odd total column:last cell in odd total column)	odd item *SD* 2.874 even item *SD* 2.901 Total *SD* 5.664
		=STDEV.S(1st cell in even total column:last cell in even total column)	
		=STDEV.S(1st cell in total column:last cell in total column)	
5.	Enter odd *SD* into any cell to the far right at the top, say M1	Type in odd total score *SD*	2.874
6.	Square odd *SD* (use cell M2)	=M1*M1	8.259876
7.	Enter even *SD* into cell M3	Type in even total score *SD*	2.901
8.	Square even *SD* (use cell M4)	=M4*M4	8.415801
9.	Add M2 and M4 (use cell M5)	=M2+M4	16.675677
10.	Enter total *SD* (use cell M6)	Type in total score *SD*	5.664
11.	Square total *SD* (use call M7)	=M7*M7	32.080896
12.	Divide M5 by M7 (use M8)	=M5/M7	0.51980085
13.	Subtract M8 from 1 (use M9)	=1−M8	0.48019915
14.	Multiply 2 and M9	=2*M9	0.960398301

Cronbach's alpha = .96

How would you interpret the resulting reliability coefficient? This reliability coefficient is high, suggesting that only 4% of the variance is measurement error, whereas 96% is meaningful variance. Whatever construct the questionnaire items is capturing (learners' evaluation of an instructor?), the instrument is doing it consistently.

STUDENT WORKBOOK
CHAPTER 9

VALIDITY AND VALIDATION

TEST YOURSELF

Working alone or with a study partner, ask and answer these questions:

1. What are some questions raised by the idea of test validity?

2. Why would both test reliability and validity be important to someone doing research?

3. What is test validity? What is test validation?

4. What are three examples of constructs? Where can more examples be found in the book?

5. What are some characteristics of test validity, as seen from the 1960s to the 1980s?

6. What is face validity?

7. What is content validity?

8. What is construct validity?

9. What are some characteristics of test validity, as seen from 1990s to the present?

10. What are the four quadrants included in Kunnan's 1998 validity model?

11. What is one validation strategy suggested by Quadrants A, B, C, and D?

12. What is test washback?

DISCUSSION QUESTIONS

1. There are quite a few examples of constructs given in this chapter and in the book. To what extent do you think a construct is something we just make up? What makes you think so?

2. Clearly, thinking about test validity has gone through some changes over time. How do you account for the changes?

3. Norris comments that day-to-day school tests may not need to be perfectly reliable. What are some reasons why that might be the case?

4. What do you think accounts for the lack of comfort testing specialists apparently feel about doing research in Quadrants B, C, and D of Kunnan's model?

APPLICATION TASKS

1. A teacher colleague tells you he or she has written an end-of-chapter vocabulary test, and asks you how to plan a test validation project. Explain Kunnan's four quadrants and then suggest validation strategies from one of the quadrants.

2. Apply the test washback model we adapted from Saif (2006) (Textbook Figure 9.2) course context, causes based on test design, and applied causes) to a test in a class you are currently teaching. If you are not currently teaching a second language course, ask a colleague for permission to apply the model to a test they are using.

3. Locate a test validation report in a second language teaching or testing journal. Explain the report to your classmates, paying par-

ticular attention to the way the authors state their understanding of test validity.

4. What are at least three group differences you can name in one second language class you are currently teaching? How would you respond to these groups differences in a high-stakes test in your course?

TEST YOURSELF ANSWERS

Working alone or with a study partner, ask and answer these questions:

1. What are some questions raised by the idea of test validity?
   Does a test measure what a test writer thinks it measures? Does a test measure what a test user thinks it measures? Can we make appropriate and fair decisions with a test?

2. Why would both test reliability and validity be important to someone doing research?
   If you use a test to show whether learners improved or changed in some way, the test should be reliable. A reliable test will result in scores that are the most accurate representation of learners' knowledge, skills, and abilities. A test should also be valid for what the researcher wishes to know. A test on reading can be reliable, but if the researcher wishes to know whether learners changed in terms of their listening skills, reading test scores should not be used to explore that. The same applies to a questionnaire. A questionnaire can be reliable, like a test, but if it does not have items that match the learner attitudes, knowledge, etc. researchers wish to know about, then the questionnaire is not valid for the purpose the researcher intends for it.

3. What is test validity? What is test validation?
   Test validity refers to the trustworthiness and soundness of scores from a test in terms of what we wish to know about learners. Doe the test match what we wish to know? Test validation is the process by which a TREE makes arguments, based on evidence, that a test has validity, and that the scores are used appropriately.

4. What are three examples of constructs? Where can more examples be found in the book?
   Learners' ability to use a variety of topic-related vocabulary for communicative purposes.

Learners' ability to write a coherent paragraph about a topic or experience.
Learners' ability to use strategic competence while answering questions.
Learners' ability to interpret meaning in a recorded conversation between friends about a club meeting and other social engagements. Chapters 2 and 4 are just two other chapters with examples of constructs.

5. What are some characteristics of test validity, as seen from the 1960s to the 1980s?
   Validity is a characteristic of a test. A test is either valid or not valid.
   Test reliability and validity are two separate concepts. There is face validity, content validity, criterion validity, and construct validity. They are four distinct aspects of validity.

6. What is face validity?
   The extent a test looks like a test, and is accepted as a "good" test by multiple stakeholders.

7. What is content validity?
   The extent to which a test samples the content and activities done in a course curriculum.

8. What is construct validity?
   The extent to which a test measures the ability, skill, knowledge, or attitude the TREE is interested. Some would refer to this as a psychometric understanding of test validity.

9. What are some characteristics of test validity, as seen from 1990s to the present?
   Validity is a characteristic not of a test, but of test score interpretation. Is the interpretation of the scores appropriate and trustworthy?
   Validity is partial, conditional upon the test administration, and never complete.
   Reliability is a precondition for validity and is part of validity.
   Construct validity is a single concept standing in for face validity and other validity types taken for granted from the 1960s to the 1980s.

10. What are the four quadrants included in Kunnan's 1998 validity model?
    Score interpretation; Test usefulness; Stakeholder values; Social, learning, and teaching consequences

Second Language Testing for Student Evaluation and Classroom Research 119

11. What is one validation strategy suggested by Quadrants A, B, C, and D?
    Quadrant A: An account of colleagues' suggestions for a statement of construct and sample items.
    Quadrant B: Notes that the test design was changed to accommodate learner group differences.
    Quadrant C: Notes on feedback sought and received from the learners and other stakeholder groups.
    Quadrant D: An account of colleagues' reactions to and comments about a causal model for washback on a specific test.

12. What is test washback?
    The presumption that a test will affect learners', teachers', and other stakeholders' behaviors, plans, and decisions.

DISCUSSION QUESTIONS ANSWERS

1. There are quite a few examples of constructs given in this chapter and in the book. To what extent do you think a construct is something we just make up? What makes you think so?
   By this point, after working with other chapters in the book, we hope you see constructs as something that the test maker makes up or states. But we also hope that you understand that current theories, and current and commonly held conceptions of language learning and language ability are consulted. In other words, we state a construct, but we draw upon our education and reading in order to define and state the construct.

2. Clearly, thinking about test validity has gone through some changes over time. How do you account for the changes?
   We cannot predict what you will say given the history and enduring concerns we presented. We would add that there seems to be a stronger emphasis on learners, and the need for educators to understand that tests have consequences, whether good or bad, for anyone who takes a test. We think this increases our responsibility to design and use good tests that provides scores that we put to an appropriate use.

3. Norris comments that day-to-day school tests may not need to be perfectly reliable. What are some reasons why that might be the case?
   You may have your own ideas on this. We could not comment at length on this, but we would ask that you consider all the ways that

tests or quizzes were used in your classes in the past year, whether as a teacher or a learner. Many test purposes, such as diagnosis (testing for the purposes of giving feedback), may require real-time, subjective responses from teachers. These responses may seem unreliable in that they cannot be quantified. Yet such commentary has a place in learners' classroom experiences.

4. What do you think accounts for the lack of comfort testing specialists apparently feel about doing research in Quadrants B, C, and D of Kunnan's model?

We think that many teachers and educators do not feel they have testing expertise. They may equate testing expertise with the ability to work with constructs, and with feeling at ease with numbers and data analysis. That said, Quadrants B, C, and D also require the ability to plan some basic research and work with descriptive statistics, none of which is beyond the ability of any educator. And, some of the validation strategies suggested in Quadrants B, C, and D may seem more relevant to many TREEs working in classroom and school settings.

APPLICATION TASKS

1. A teacher colleague tells you he or she has written an end-of-chapter vocabulary test and asks you how to plan a test validation project. Explain Kunnan's four quadrants and then suggest strategies from one of the quadrants.

To answer this, we suggest you study the model and create practical examples of the quadrants to help make the explanations more clear. Although we offer strategies for all four quadrants in the chapter, perhaps you can generate a few more. Ask your classmates or your instructor as to whether the strategies make sense or whether they belong to a quadrant. You may find that the model adapted from Kunnan (1998) does not necessarily cover all possible validation strategies! See commentary from Norris, for example, or O'Sullivan and Weir.

2. Apply the test washback model we adapted from Saif (2006) (course context, causes based on test design, and applied causes) to a test in a class you are currently teaching. If you are not currently teaching a second-language course, ask a colleague for permission to apply the model to a test they are using.

You may wish to focus on what evidence you could collect that would tell you whether your various causes were in fact test-related causes of changes in learners' or teachers' plans or behavior. How would you know whether learners changed the way they studied, or how much time they spent on activities related to the test? Give your first draft of your application study to your instructor or a classmate for feedback.

3. Locate a test validation report in a second language teaching or testing journal. Explain the report to your classmates, paying particular attention to the way the authors state their understanding of test validity.
We suggest the following journals and other sources of test reports. You can find websites for these journals and at the very least can look at their Tables of Contents or do a search within the journal. Do not be surprised if a validation report is not actually called that. If you find the citation for an article or report, then you can ask your library to retrieve the article for you. If your library does not offer interlibrary loan, then you can ask a colleague to retrieve the article for you, if they work for a school that has a library with retrieval rights.

Language Testing

Language Assessment Quarterly

Assessing Writing

Language Testing in Asia

Modern Language Journal

Foreign Language Annals

TESOL Quarterly

TESOL Journal

JALT Journal

System

International Language Testing Association (this is not a journal but rather an organization that has publications such as books and monographs)
Educational Testing Service (this is not a journal but rather a company that has publications such as monographs)
Cambridge Michigan Language Assessments (this is not a journal but rather a company—it is not clear from their current website whether they have monographs, reports, etc., for purchase)
Center for Advanced Research on Language Acquisition (this is not a journal but rather a research center that has publications such as monographs)

4. What are at least three group differences you can name in one second language class you are currently teaching? How would you respond to these groups differences in a high-stakes test in your course?

    We provide some examples in the chapter but you can probably think of more. You might show your list to colleagues and to an administrator in your school for comment, and ask them for suggestions. Create some provisional responses, and at the very least, plan to check for group differences in scores.

STUDENT WORKBOOK
CHAPTER 10

STANDARD SETTING AND CUT SCORES

TEST YOURSELF

Working alone or with a study partner, ask and answer these questions:

1. What is a cut score?

2. What is a cut score used for?

3. What is standard setting?

4. What is a false positive?

5. What is a false negative?

6. Can you describe the norm-referenced cut score methods, both types I and II?

7. Can you describe the criterion-referenced cut score method?

8. Do the norm-referenced and criterion-referenced cut score methods involve standard setting?

9. What are some of the pieces of logic behind standard setting?

10. What is a C– student?

11. Can you describe the yes/no standard setting method?

12. Can you describe the direct consensus standard setting method?

13. How is the contrasting groups method different than the yes/no method and the direct consensus method?

14. Can you describe the contrasting groups standard setting method?

15. In what circumstances would a TREE use Griffee's Statistical Method?

DISCUSSION QUESTIONS

1. Referring to the conversation between two students at the beginning of the chapter, suppose you are the teacher and the student has come to you to discuss his or her grade. Depending on the standard setting and cut score method you would choose, how would you explain the B grade for this student?

2. Choose a cut score method or a standard setting method and focus on the issues and concerns listed for that method. Can you add anything to the list?

3. For that same list, what are some ways you can answer the issues and concerns?

4. How would you go about persuading a colleague or administrator that some standard setting method should go along with setting cut scores on a high-stakes test?

APPLICATION TASK

1. Pick out a test that you have used recently. Or ask a colleague for a test he or she used recently. Find two to three expert raters, perhaps from another school (do not leak the test items if the test will be

used again). Use the yes/no method or the direct consensus method to find a cut score for the test.

2. Using the same test for application task #1, work with the expert rater panel and use the yes/no method or the direct consensus method to get standards for A, B, C, and F grades on the test. This means setting four cut scores.

3. Find a book chapter or an article that describes standard setting. Examples are Cizek (2001, 2006), Hambleton (2008), and Hambleton and Sireci (1997) but also:

Baron, P., & Papageorgiou, S. (2016). *Setting language proficiency score requirements for English-as-s-second-language placement decisions in secondary education*. Princeton, NJ: ETS Research Report Series: Educational Testing Service. ISSN: 2330–8516.

Bueno-Alastuey, M., Laborda, J., Alcon, A., & Agullo, G. (2014). Setting standards for the foreign language speaking tasks of the new Baccalaureate General Test. *Theory and Practice in Language Studies, 4*(9), 1763–1769.

Oregon Department of Education (2010). *Second language standards*. Available: http://www.ode.state.or.us/teachlearn/subjects/secondlanguages/standards/second-language-all-in-one.pdf

Tannenbaum, R., & Cho, Y. (2014). Critical factors to consider in evaluating standard-setting methods to map language test scores to frameworks of language proficiency. *Language Assessment Quarterly, 11*, 233–249.

Retrieve the chapter, article, or report, and prepare a presentation that describes the standard setting being used, what it is for, and how it was done. Some of these publications are more about how to do standard setting than they describe an actual standard setting procedure. Nonetheless such publications are useful. Be sure to add at least three additional points about standard setting that are not included in Chapter 10 of this book.

TEST YOURSELF ANSWERS

1. What is a cut score?
   A cut score is a dividing score above which students are one status and below which is student another status.

2. What is a cut score used for?
   Cut scores can be used for pass/fail decisions. The cut score is the lowest possible pass point. Cut scores are also used for grading decisions

such as A, B, C, and so on on a test. Above a certain cut score, learners will get an A, and below that, a B, and so on

3. What is standard setting?
The process by which a cut score is set. Most methods require a combination of mathematical work and human judgment.

4. What is a false positive?
A learner who passed or got a high grade, but who should not have.

5. What is a false negative?
A learner who failed or got a low score, but who should not have.

6. Can you describe the norm-referenced cut score methods, both types I and II?
In norm-referenced method I, the top scoring 50% of learners pass, and the bottom scoring 50% of learners fail. In a grade situation, the next top scoring 10% get a B, the next top scoring 10% get a C, and so on. In norm-referenced method II, the mean score is calculated. Learners who score three standard deviations above the mean gets As, those scoring two standard deviations above the mean get B, and so on.

7. Can you describe the criterion-referenced cut score method?
Depending on the number of items on a test, a TREE sets equal increments of points to determine grade bands from the highest possible score learners can get on the test. For a 50-item test, anyone getting from 45 to 50 points gets an A, 40–44 gets a B, and so on.

8. Do the norm- and criterion-referenced cut score methods involve standard setting?
Not really. The cut scores are set using math and some implicit ideas about normal distributions. Even the criterion-referenced cut score method, where learners are not compared to each other, assumes a kind of normal distribution in that only learners getting nearly every item right should get an A.

9. What are some of the pieces of logic behind standard setting?
Some standard setting methods assume a hypothesized C– minus student and ask human raters to consider how well a C– student would do on test items, or subtests. Some standard setting methods require a consensus among panelists, or multiple rounds of rating. Most important, standard setting methods require panelists and TREEs

to match test scores with what learners know and can do. This means that TREEs and/or panelists are committing to deciding what is important for learners to know and do, and how well they need to know and do those things for some use. Finally, cut scores coming out of most standard setting processes can be carried forward and used for future test administrations, at least for a few years. Standard setting represents accumulated knowledge that can be used for program planning, and planning for teaching and curricula.

10. What is a C– student?
    A learner who is minimally competent, came to class and tried, and got something out of the course but is no star.

11. Can you describe the yes/no standard setting method?
    Panelists examine individual test items or test tasks and decide whether they think a C– can answer each item correctly or do the task.

12. Can you describe the direct consensus standard setting method?
    Working together in a meeting, panelists look at subtests from a test and decide how many items out of the subtest a C– student could answer. Their answers are put on the board, and panelists discuss until the reach a consensus.

13. How is the contrasting groups method different than the yes/no method and the direct consensus method?
    The contrasting groups method uses scores from learners who have already taken the test, whereas the yes/no method and the direct consensus method rely on judgments based on test items, not learners' actual test scores.

14. Can you describe the contrasting groups standard setting method?
    The learners are split into two groups, masters and nonmasters. The two score distributions of the two groups are put on top of each other as two histograms and the place where the lower end of the masters' distribution and the upper end of the nonmasters' distribution is the proposed cut point.

15. In what circumstances would a TREE use Griffee's Statistical Method?
    When you have existing data, can reliably put learners into masters and non-masters group based on other test scores, and when there is no time to put together a panel of experts.

DISCUSSION QUESTIONS

1. Referring to the conversation between two students at the beginning of the chapter, suppose you are the teacher and the student has come to you to discuss his or her grade. Depending on the standard setting and cut score method you would choose, how would you explain the B grade for this student?
   Clearly your reasons to give the student will have more impact if you have used a standard setting procedure to set the cut scores. When you can relate test scores with course content it become more clear what the learner still needs to work on to get an A.

2. Choose a cut score method or a standard setting method and focus on the issues and concerns listed for that method. Can you add anything to the list?
   We cannot predict what you will say but hope you will share your ideas with us.

3. For that same list, what are some ways you can answer the issues and concerns?
   For most concerns there are reasonable answers or solutions that we can offer, as long as our reasons are clearly described, and defensible. We would point out one issue and that is whether expert raters could set standards for A, B, C, and D grades on a test. While we think it is more complicated than simply identifying a C- student, we think that with focused discussion, teachers are well able to describe A learners, B learners, and so on and relate these descriptions to test items, test tasks, and test subtests.

4. How would you go about persuading a colleague or administrator that some standard setting method should go along with setting cut scores on a high-stakes test?
   We have a few suggestions: Point out how most cut scores are set with reference to the idea of a normal distribution, which leaves out any organized thinking on what test scores mean. You can also point out that standard setting would help match test scores to what learners know and can do, and may bring about greater consensus among colleagues about the program and courses.

STUDENT WORKBOOK
CHAPTER 11

TESTS AND TEACHING

TEST YOURSELF

Working alone or with a study partner, ask and answer these questions:

1. What does the term diagnosis mean, and what does it have to do with tests and teaching?

2. Why might norm-referenced tests be disconnected from teaching? What about criterion-referenced tests?

3. From a teacher's point of view what are some reasons for a disconnect between tests and teaching?

4. What is test effect? How does it work?

5. What is a pedagogically worthwhile test?

6. According to the commentary on formative assessment and pedagogically worthwhile tests, what kind of feedback is most useful to learners?

7. What is the zone of proximal development?

8. What is dynamic assessment?

9. What are some of the challenges to use dynamic assessment?

DISCUSSION QUESTIONS

1. One of the early points in the chapter is that teachers may use tests in general ways, such as reminding students to study, and deciding grades. A TREE may even work quite hard to write and use tests that have content validity. But using tests directly for teaching and learning may be something different altogether. Given the sources, suggestions, and models given in the chapter, what do you think? Why so?

2. Does a test have to have content validity (alignment between test content and test item formats, and the course curriculum) to be used in the ways described in the chapter? Why or why not?

3. Diagnosis has been described as one of the main decisions that tests can be used for, in addition to placement, achievement, and so on. In your experience as a teacher or learner, have you seen a test used for diagnosis? What was the form of the feedback given to learners? Were the test results used for other teaching actions?

4. Evaluate the reasons given for a lack of alignment between tests and teaching. Which do you think is the most convincing reason? Which reasons do you feel less convinced about? Are there reasons you know of that are not given in the chapter?

5. In the commentary on test effect, it almost sounds as though it is enough to simply give learners many tests. Is that the case? Or are there additional steps that need to be used?

6. What additional help with dynamic assessment would you need before you could use it in a class with 20 learners? What specific questions do you have? How would you go about finding answers to your questions?

7. Can you think of any objections your colleagues or supervisors might have if you used test effect, pedagogically worthwhile tests, or dynamic assessment to more closely align your tests and teaching? How would you deal with their objections, if they had any?

APPLICATION TASKS

1. This task builds on the application task from the Student Workbook Chapter 2 on test item formats (TIFs).

    Either review the information you already have from the Student Workbook Chapter 2 application task or start fresh with a criterion-referenced test or quiz used in your courses or program.

    Find a test, describe it, and bring it to class.

    What is the name of the test? _____

    What is the name of the course the test is use _____

    What is the name of the course the test is used in? _____

    What are the objectives of the course this test was designed to capture?
    _____
    _____

    How many items does the test have?_____

    How many TIFs were used? _____

    TIF #1 name_____ What was the percent of use?____

    TIF #2 name_____ What was the percent of use?____

    TIF #3 name_____ What was the percent of use?____

Select one of the TIFs above. What knowledge or skill (the construct) is the TIF measuring?

_____

_____

_____

What are the strong and weak points of the TIF?

_____

_____

In Sudent Workbook Table 11.1 please evaluate and comment on at least two TIFs in terms of the concepts in Chapter 11 on tests and teaching:

Table 11.1.
Student Workbook Connecting TIFs to Testing and Teaching Concepts

Concepts/	TIF #1: _____	TIF #1	TIF #2: _____	TIF #2
	Easy or difficult to apply the items to the concept? How so?	What is the first step you can take to apply the items to the concept?	Easy or difficult to apply the items to the concept? How so?	What is the first step you can take to apply the items to the concept?
Diagnosis: Giving feedback to learners				

(Table continues on next page)

Table 11.1.
TIFs to Testing and Teaching Concepts (Continued)

Concepts	TIF #1: _____ Easy or difficult to apply the items to the concept? How so?	TIF #1 What is the first step you can take to apply the items to the concept?	TIF #2: _____ Easy or difficult to apply the items to the concept? How so?	TIF #2 What is the first step you can take to apply the items to the concept?
Diagnosis: Re-teach material				
Diagnosis: Schedule review sessions for material				
Test effect				
Pedagogically worthwhile tests				

(Table continues on next page)

Table 11.1.
TIFs to Testing and Teaching Concepts (Continued)

Concepts	TIF #1: _____ Easy or difficult to apply the items to the concept? How so?	TIF #1 What is the first step you can take to apply the items to the concept?	TIF #2: _____ Easy or difficult to apply the items to the concept? How so?	TIF #2 What is the first step you can take to apply the items to the concept?
Formative assessment				
Open-book test				
Dynamic assessment				

2. Feedback to learners appears to be an important theme in this chapter. This application task focuses on performance tests. Find a performance test, along with criteria, used in your course or program. Find also two or three spoken or written samples of learners' work and score them. Work up written feedback, or scripts for spoken feedback, for the learners that are descriptive, and suggestive of how the learners can move forward. If you do not have a performance test, here are some links with performance test criteria. Some of them have writing samples.

Writing samples from K–12 ESL learners: http://www.learnalberta.ca/content/eslapb/writing_samples.html

Sample tasks and criteria with scales for writing and speaking, and abbreviated writing samples in German:http://carla.umn.edu/assessment/MLPA/pdfs/Speaking_Writing_Tasks_Guide.pdf

Sample criteria and scales for the French writing test listed above: http://www.nysedregents.org/loteslp/french/slp-french-rg-610p.pdf

3. This task focuses on test effect. Follow these steps:

   a. Read the passage once:

   Over ten thousand years ago, the southern high plains of West Texas were inhabited by Paleo-Americans, who hunted bison and other animals. They established temporary camps based on where they hunted, and then prepared the animals as food. There are multiple sites in the area that have been investigated by archaeologists. One of the best places to see this kind of campsite is Landmark Lakes in Lubbock, Texas, that has a nature walk and an attached museum that interprets the lives of these Paleo-Americans. These people were ancient and unnamed, and yet they left enough traces of their hunting techniques and other aspects of their lives, to tell modern-day visitors something about them.

   Many visitors to the area are surprised that this part of Texas, which seems flat and dry and grassy, has so many sites created by these ancient people. Some scholars believe the climate may have been a little wetter when these ancient people hunted in the area. Nonetheless, they lived and survived here for many generations. And, even today, the high southern plains support an abundance of wildlife, and of course, modern-day humans.

   It is interesting to note that archaeology, the study of long-gone people, has controversy. One controversy has to do with whether these ancient hunters are ancestors of 19th century and modern-day American Indians, or whether these are different people altogether. In some readings on the ancient people of West Texas, they are called "Paleo-Indians" (related to modern-day American Indians) while other readings insist on the term "Paleo-Americans" (not related to modern-day American Indians). Without bones of these ancient hunters, and comparison DNA samples from modern-day American Indians, it would be difficult to know the relationships of these different groups to each other.

   b. Using a separate piece of paper, write everything you remember about the passage without looking at the passage.

c. Compare your writing sample to the passage. Note down the gaps between your writing sample and the passage.

d. Let two or three days pass. Then read the passage again.

e. Using a seperate piece of paper, write everything you remember about the passage without looking at the passage.

f. Compare your first writing sample with your second writing sample. Which is longer? Which has more detail? How do you account for any differences?

The "test" used in this test effect application task is a writing recall test, which is a kind of performance test. What are other test item formats that could be used with this passage that would take advantage of test effect? How could the different test item formats be used in your teaching to aid in learners' memory retrieval?Hint: Think about memory retrieval.

TEST YOURSELF ANSWERS

1. What does the term diagnosis mean, and what does it have to do with tests and teaching?
   Diagnosis is one of the main decisions a test is used for, in addition to placement, admission, or achievement. Scores and feedback from a test used for diagnosis are used by teachers to decide whether to teach part of a course again, do additional review sessions, and offer learners feedback for self-directed study. It also appears, based on this chapter, that teachers can use learners' performances on a test as a basis for instruction, and as direct assistance while learners attempt to answer the test questions or do the test task.

2. Why might norm-referenced tests be disconnected from teaching? What about criterion-referenced tests?
   NRTs are by design unrelated to the curriculum of any particular course or program. CRTs and performance tests may have more relationship to a course or program, but if the learners' scores or performances are not used for detailed feedback upon which additional study or teaching can be planned and done, there is greater danger of a disconnect.

3. From a teacher's point of view what are some reasons for a disconnect between tests and teaching?
   We list a number of reasons, including:
   - Tests may be seen as an afterthought to the main job of teaching
   - Making tests and teaching may seem to require different sets of skills and thought
   - Tests may give learners anxiety, and may present potential battlegrounds between teachers and learners
   - Teachers may be uneasy with the values of learners toward tests
   - New teachers or teachers in training may not get enough guidance to apply their theories and skills to writing tests
   - Some schools value testing and teaching learners on grammar and vocabulary points
   - Teachers may believe they lack the expertise to write psychometrically sophisticated tests, like the sort of tests schools may buy from companies
   - Some schools may value commercially bought tests, and teachers may feel they have to teach to such tests
   - Some teachers may be in position where, if their learners do not do well on commercially purchased tests, they will lose their jobs

4. What is test effect? How does it work?
   Test effect is the idea that taking a test increases learning more than taking notes or studying. Test effect may work through memory retrieval.

5. What is a pedagogically worthwhile test?
   A pedagogically worthwhile test is a test with test items and test item formats a teacher would be comfortable teaching. A pedagogically worthwhile test would get learners to apply what they know, and engage in reasoning and using their skills doing realistic, ordinary things.

6. According to the commentary on formative assessment and pedagogically worthwhile tests, what kind of feedback is most useful to learners?
   Feedback should be descriptive, and point to specific areas in knowledge and skills needing improvement. The feedback should help learners see a gap between what they can currently do and what they need to do. The feedback should point to a way forward for learners.

7. What is the zone of proximal development?
   ZPD is the difference between a learner's actual development and their potential development, in other words where learning can happen with the help of a teacher, colleague, or classmate.

8. What is dynamic assessment?
   A form of testing that measures what learners currently know (static testing) plus what learners know through direct mediation, such as focused, sustained instruction, or supplying hints while learners problem-solve in class.

9. What are some of the challenges to use dynamic assessment?
   It is not clear how direct, systematic, sustained interactions between an instructor and one learner can be accomplished with typical classes of twenty or more learners. It is not clear how teachers would develop a methodology of doing systematic interactions with learners based on the task. It is also not clear how teachers would select tasks that would be within learners' ZPDs.

DISCUSSION QUESTIONS ANSWERS

1. One of the early points in the chapter is that teachers may use tests in general ways, such as reminding students to study, and deciding grades. A TREE may even work quite hard to write and use tests that have content validity. But using tests directly for teaching and learning may be something different altogether. Given the sources, suggestions, and models given in the chapter, what do you think? Why so?
   We are not sure what you will say, but we would point out a few things. First, making a classroom test that has content validity is an accomplishment. It means that test item formats are similar to what learners experience in class, and that the test items test the same content, and in the same proportion, as to what learners experience in class. Second, we think teachers may follow a "default" pattern of giving learners periodic tests, and reminding students to study, without actually using the tests for actual instruction or to give descriptive feedback to learners. This chapter focuses on how tests themselves, and the act of testing, can be used for teaching and learning.

2. Does a test have to have content validity (alignment between test content and test item formats, and the course curriculum) in order to be used in the ways described in the chapter? Why or why not?
   We think that a test with content validity will be much easier for teachers to plan and do instruction from. We point to the test effect study by Leeming (2002) where he gave daily practice quizzes that mirrored the test item formats and content used in the final exam for the course.

3. Diagnosis has been described as one of the main decisions that tests can be used for, in addition to placement, achievement, etc. In your experience as a teacher or learner, have you seen a test used for diagnosis? What was the form of the feedback given to learners? Were the test results used for other teaching actions?
We are not sure what you will say. It might be easy to think that we have seen tests being used for diagnosis, but we wonder the extent to which learners' test results are used to plan teaching. We think some teachers may have trouble with the idea of responding with instruction to individual learners' problems, and that they may instead feel they have to work with some implicit ideas that addresses the "majority" of learners. We also wonder whether feedback to learners is simply in the form of scores, as opposed to descriptive prose feedback with suggestions for moving forward.

4. Evaluate the reasons given for a lack of alignment between tests and teaching. Which do you think is the most convincing reason? Which reasons do you feel less convinced about? Are there reasons you know of that are not given in the chapter?
It is unclear what you will say. Given your experiences, you may have many different responses. We would comment that any reasons you feel strongly about should be investigated formally through a literature search. Well-documented issues teachers have with tests and teaching may be a very good conference presentation or poster idea.

5. In the commentary on test effect, it almost sounds as though it is enough to simply give learners many tests. Is that the case? Or are there additional steps that need to be used?
We think the practice of giving many small tests is under-valued. At the same time, we have been in situations where learners want to take an NRT or performance test over and over because they do not believe their scores, or because they think they will get lucky "next time" and get the score they want. NRTs and some performance tests are probably not the best types of tests to benefit learners using test effect. NRTs have unpredictable content, and improvement on some performance tests may come slowly, depending on how broad the criteria "bands" are (see Chapter 5 on performance tests). CRTs with good content validity, and performance tests with short, specific tasks and specific criteria being focused on, may be the best to use. The literature on test effect stipulates that learners get immediate feedback after tests, that tests be frequent and short, and that tests should immediately follow instruction. The literature also stipulates reducing

learners' anxiety through several means, including telling learners the practice tests do not count toward their course grades.

6. What additional help with dynamic assessment, would you need before you could use it in a class with 20 learners? What specific questions do you have? How would you go about finding answers to your questions?

   It is uncertain what you will say, but we wonder what whole-class adaptations teachers might make to the individualized, consistent help and hints described in the dynamic assessment literature. We wonder if whole-class-help-and-hints sessions might give the appearance of learner participation and learning, but also whether learners whose ZPDs are not in the range of the help and hints are silently sitting in class without being helped. We also wonder whether whole class sessions will allow individual learners to resolve their questions and problems with learning points. Would having learners write down what they understand after the sessions help them work out what they understand and what they still do not understand? We hope that readers who are interested in dynamic assessment will look at the literature to find answers to the questions they have. There are many conference presentation ideas and research projects that can be done here.

7. Can you think of any objections your colleagues or supervisors might have if you used test effect, pedagogically worthwhile tests, or dynamic assessment to more closely align tests and teaching? How would you deal with their objections, if they had any?

   We are unsure what you will say. Some colleagues, to the extent they care what others do, may say you are teaching to the test, which is somehow thought to be bad. Other colleagues or supervisors may be concerned about the security of high-stakes end-of-semester tests. If you base instruction on the tests, will that not alert students to the test content? Sometimes answering concerns using the concept of content validity helps when discussing tests with colleagues. Also, citing learner motivation might help. We think that the mindset behind NRTs is still strong among many educators. This mindset says that tests should be unpredictable, and learners' abilities are normally distributed. This flies in the face of the mindset behind CRTs and performance tests that learners should know exactly what to expect in the test. This may yet be another source of ideas for addressing colleagues' concerns.

APPLICATION TASKS ANSWERS

1. This task builds on the application task from the student workbook for Chapter 2 on test item formats (TIFs).

   Either review the information you already have from the application task or start fresh with a criterion-referenced test or quiz used in your courses or program.

   Find a test, describe it, and bring it to class.

   What is the name of the test?
   If no name is used, then ask for the name from the test writer or create a name that accurately describes the test.

   What is the name of the course the test is used in?
   Get the precise course name.

   What are the objectives of the course this test was designed to capture?
   This can be found on the course syllabus or course description. If no objectives are named, then ask the test writer or instructors of the course about the course objectives. Examples from a first semester college-level Japanese course are:
   Students completing this course will be able to communicate orally at the ACTFL Novice.

   High level or at the Common European Framework of Reference for Languages (CEFRL) level A2.

   The student will acquire a vocabulary of about 400 words and 90 Kanji characters.

   The student will learn functional tasks such as those listed below in the specific goals.

   The student will be able to interpret, express and negotiate meaning, and communicate appropriately by using Japanese in the Japanese culture.

   How many items does the test have?
   Recall that an item is a question or statement that test candidates respond to, and where the response is scored. Thus, a test may have only two items if the TIF being used is short response or a task. A test using true/false or fill-in-the-blank TIFs may have a larger number of items.

How many TIFs were used?

Ask a classmate to check and confirm your answer.

TIF #1 name_____   What was the percent of use?____

TIF #2 name_____   What was the percent of use?____

TIF #3 name_____   What was the percent of use?____

Confirm your answers with a classmate or colleague.

Select one of the TIFs above. What knowledge or skill (the construct) is the TIF measuring?
Show the sample items to a classmate or colleague and explain what you think the construct is.

What are the strong and weak points of the TIF?
Answers can focus on several points: (a) the extent to which the TIF can capture a given construct, (b) the extent to which the TIF reflects a course objective (if the test is a classroom test designed to show students' learning), (c) the extent to which a TIF can be credibly and reliably scored, and (d) the extent to which a TIF is communicative.

In Student Workbook Table 11.2 please evaluate and comment on at least two TIFs in terms of the concepts in Chapter 11 on tests and teaching:

Table 11.2.
Student Workbook Connecting TIFs to Testing and Teaching Concepts

Concepts	TIF #1: _____	TIF #1	TIF #2: _____	TIF #2
	This should be one of the TIFs shown in Textbook Chapter 2. Easy or difficult to apply the items to the concept? How so?	What is the first step you can take to apply the items to the concept?	This should be a second TIF shown in Textbook Chapter 2. It may be that the test has only one TIF. For example, it may be a performance test. In this case, you will not be able to comment on TIF #2. Easy or difficult to apply the items to the concept? How so?	What is the first step you can take to apply the items to the concept?
Diagnosis: Giving feedback to learners	Successful completion of this task would be at least 75% of the cells in the table being completed with substantive answers.	Some readers may find it easier here to provide an example of how they would use a TIF in their teaching. Other readers may mention a specific source they could consult, including asking colleagues, looking up relevant literature, and so on.		
Diagnosis: Re-teach material				

2. Feedback to learners appears to be an important theme in this chapter. This application task focuses on performance tests. Find a performance test, along with criteria, used in your course or program. Find also two or three spoken or written samples of learners' work and score them. Work up written feedback, or scripts for spoken feedback, for the learners that are descriptive, and suggestive of how the learners can move forward. If you do not have a performance test, here are some links with performance test criteria. Some of them have writing samples.

   Show your written feedback or spoken scripts to a classmate or colleague to check whether the feedback is descriptive, and gives ideas about moving forward. The ideas should be more than "study harder" or "memorize longer," and they should be varied and specific.

3. This task focuses on test effect. Follow these steps:

   a. Read the passage once:

   f. Compare your first writing sample with your second writing sample. Which is longer? Which has more detail? Why do you think so?

   Some readers will find that the second writing sample has more detail due to repeated processing of the text and memory retrieval: reading the text previously, writing a recall of the text, and comparing the recall to the text (which would result in yet another reading of the text and additional memory retrieval).

   The "test" used in this application task is a writing recall test, which is a kind of performance test. What are other test item formats that could be used with this passage? How could the different test item formats be used in your teaching to aid in learners' memory retrieval?

   A successful answer would be at least two additional TIFs that could be used with specific suggestions the items could be used in teaching, as competitive games, group and pair testing (one learner reads a test item to another learner and checks their answer), writing short answers, and so on.

STUDENT WORKBOOK
CHAPTER 12

TESTS AND CLASSROOM RESEARCH

TEST YOURSELF

Working alone or with a study partner, ask and answer these questions:

1. What is confirmatory research?

2. What is descriptive research?

3. What is evaluation?

4. What are at least two example constructs from the chapter?

5. What should a test have, regardless of research type it is used in?

6. What are NRTs useful for in research? What are they not useful for?

7. What are CRTs useful for in research?

8. What descriptive statistics for a test should be presented in a research report?

9. What is formative evaluation? How is it different from formative assessment?

10. What can a test tell us in formative evaluation?

11. What is summative evaluation?

12. What can a test tell us in summative evaluation?

DISCUSSION QUESTIONS

1. One of our main points in the chapter is that tests must have validation evidence, and that test users must show validity evidence, in order to increase the clarity of research. How would showing validity increase the clarity of a piece of research?

2. Part of demonstrating validity of a test is stating the construct for the test. Do you think it is enough to simply know the construct statement, or would you need to see the actual test as well?

3. How is classroom research different from the test validation research described in Chapter 9 on test validity?

APPLICATION TASKS

1. In Textbook Table 12.3, we list 15 categories of information needed for reporting test results in classroom research. Evaluate one of the studies shown in Textbook Table 12.1. Does the author or authors include information on all of the categories? If there are omissions, do you think that detracts from your understanding of the test results? Of from your understanding of the research? Why or why not?

2. Many research reports may show little change in learners' test scores. This is sometimes described using language such as "the results failed to reject the null hypothesis" and "there appeared to be little change." Retrieve a research article in which a test has been used where the researcher reports little or no change, according to test results. Could the lack of positive results be due to issues with the test, as opposed to the research treatments, or the theory, the research was based on? In other words, perhaps there may have

been changes in learners, but which the test did not detect. Give reasons, based on the report.

TEST YOURSELF ANSWERS

1. What is confirmatory research?
   A type of research that first identifies a theory and then proceeds to test it by gathering data that either strengthens or confirms the theory or weakens or disconfirms the theory.

2. What is descriptive research?
   Refers to research that is oriented toward extensive use of data that allow conclusions to emerge.

3. What is evaluation?
   The process by which a program or course is judged to be adequate or operating effectively. Evaluation is also used to revitalize and improve programs and courses.

4. What are at least two example constructs from the chapter?
   There are examples in Textbook Table 12.1, one of which is "reading comprehension of main ideas, supporting details, details, and inference of an L2 text." Constructs for each of the research reports in the table are listed.

5. What should a test have, regardless of research type it is used in?
   Tests should have validity, and corresponding validation evidence. Readers need to have a clear idea of the construct, which is part of validation. If the construct is not clear, or if the test does not have items that capture the construct, or if the construct or test is not sensitive to learner changes relevant to the research, then it is not possible to know whether the test results mean anything.

6. What are NRTs useful for in research? What are they not useful for?
   NRTs can be used to describe learners at the outset of a study. They can also be used to show that learner groups are at some level of equivalence at the beginning of a study. NRTs are not effective to show changes in learners, particularly over short periods of time.

7. What are CRTs useful for in research?
   CRTs are useful to show learner achievement and change over time, assuming the CRT is valid and also relevant to the research treatments, instruction, etc.

8. What descriptive statistics for a test should be presented in a research report?
   Mean, median, mode, standard deviation, minimum and maximum scores, skewness, standard error of skewness, kurtosis, and standard error of kurtosis.

9. What is formative evaluation? How is it different from formative assessment?
   Formative evaluation is research for the purpose of improving, illuminating, and clarifying how well a course moves learners to the course objectives. Formative assessment refers to an educational movement in which learners are tested frequently, and then given direct and descriptive feedback based on the tests.

10. What can a test tell us in formative evaluation?
    Tests can inform TREEs as to what learners are achieving or what they are not doing as well on at a given point in a course. This information can be used to plan different instruction, more review, etc. Tests can also provide important information about a course curriculum, revealing the thinking and priorities of the test users.

11. What is summative evaluation?
    An assessment of a course or student at the end of a course, done for purposes of illumination and improvement of a course, but also for reasons of accountability.

12. What can a test tell us in summative evaluation?
    Whether learners have met the course objectives. Tests can also be used to judge the course objectives themselves. If learners did not meet the objectives, what needs to be changed? Or do the objectives themselves need to be changed?

DISCUSSION QUESTIONS

1. One of our main points in the chapter is that tests must have validation evidence, and test users must show validity evidence to increase the clarity of research. How would showing validity increase the clarity of a piece of research?
   Readers need to have a clear idea of the construct, which is major part of validity and validation. If the construct is not clear, or if the test does not have items that capture the construct, or if the construct or test is not sensitive to learner changes relevant to the research, then

it is not possible to know whether the test results mean anything. Validation evidence can help us to know what the researchers think they are measuring. We can then judge more clearly for ourselves whether the tests match the treatments, or whatever the learners are doing during the study. If we can say yes, the test appears valid for the research, then the test results will be more clearly interpretable. "Right, it appears the treatments did not work" or "Learners really did change, perhaps because of the treatments."

2. Part of demonstrating validity of a test is stating the construct for the test. Do you think it is enough to simply know the construct statement, or would you need to see the actual test as well?
We are not sure what you will say. But actually seeing the test or representative test items, and comparing them to the stated test constructs, might be convincing. This is related to our commentary in Chapter 4 on communicative language theory that many TREEs may state their test constructs as "communicative competence" but then use test item formats that do not capture communicative competence (see Figure 4.2 and Table 4.5). A comparison between the construct statement and sample test items would tell us quickly whether they match.

3. How is classroom research different from the test validation research described in Chapter 9 on test validity?
Classroom research focuses on understanding what happens in classrooms in terms of instruction, learner activities and their interaction with each other, etc. Many data collection instruments can be used, such as interviews, observations, and so on. Test validation research may also focus on learners' interactions, and so on, but for the purpose of understanding the effect of those interactions on learners' test performances. Tests are central in such research, not merely a means of collecting data as it would be in classroom research. The main object of test validation research is, among other things, to understand potential effects of administration, design, learners' values, and so on on learners' test scores and performances. Note also test washback research, which may detect effects in classrooms, but once again the test is central to the research, not simply a means of collecting data.

APPLICATION TASKS

1. In Texbook Table 12.3, we list 15 categories of information needed for reporting test results in classroom research. Evaluate one of the

studies shown in Textbook Table 12.1. Does the author or authors include information on all of the categories? If there are omissions, do you think that detracts from your understanding of the test results? From your understanding of the research? Why or why not?
It is unclear which research report you will select. One thing you might find is that the actual tests on some of the studies have not been provided. Some authors or editors may not know it should be included, or they may think there is not enough space. Yet good practice supports including at least sample items. Note the British Academy and Economic and Social Research Council IRIS database of data-collection instruments, including tests, which are submitted to the database managers on publication of a research report: www.iris-database.org We think there is a growing consensus that tests used in research, especially tests designed to show change, should accompany the research report. Other readers may be more sensitive to the omission of descriptive statistics or histograms, whereas others, including one of the authors here, are sensitive to the test range being omitted. Without test range, it is hard to get an idea of how much learners actually improved or changed.

2. Many research reports may show little change in learners' test scores. This is sometimes described using language such as "the results failed to reject the null hypothesis" and "there appeared to be little change." Retrieve a research article in which a test has been used where the researcher reports little or no change, according to test results. Could the lack of positive results be due to issues with the test, as opposed to the research treatments, or the theory the research was based on? In other words, perhaps there may have been changes in learners, but which the test did not detect. Give reasons, based on the report.
We are not sure which report you will retrieve. Successful completion of this task would include a full citation for the report (such as those found in Table 12.1), a quotation from the report that no effect was found, and at least two paragraphs with your speculations as to the reason for no effect. Rule out problems with the test, first. If you cannot comment adequately on the test because validation information is missing, be sure to say so. Also, was the treatment intensive enough, for long enough? Some treatments may be effective but in some confirmatory research the treatment is only done a few times. Some answers to the issue of "no effect" can be surprisingly commonsense.

www.ingramcontent.com/pod-product-compliance
Lightning Source LLC
Chambersburg PA
CBHW051102230426
43667CB00013B/2407